Multiliteracies

Beyond Text and the Written Word

A volume in
Landscapes of Education
William H. Schubert and Ming Fang He, *Series Editors*

Multiliteracies

Beyond Text and the Written Word

edited by

Eugene F. Provenzo, Jr.
Amanda Goodwin
Miriam Lipsky
Sheree Sharpe

IAP

INFORMATION AGE PUBLISHING, INC.
Charlotte, NC • www.infoagepub.com

Library of Congress Cataloging-in-Publication Data

Multiliteracies beyond text and the written word / edited by Eugene F. Provenzo, Jr. ... [et al.].
p. cm. – (Landscapes of education)
Includes bibliographical references.
ISBN 978-1-61735-342-0 (pbk.) – ISBN 978-1-61735-343-7 (hardcover) – ISBN 978-1-61735-344-4 (e-book)
1. Visual literacy–United States. 2. Media literacy–United States. 3. Literacy–Social aspects–United States. 4. Computers and literacy–United States. I. Provenzo, Eugene F.
LB1068.M85 2011
302.2'244–dc22

2010052690

Printed and bound by CPI Group (UK) Ltd, Croydon, CR0 4YY

Contents

Series Foreword

Landscapes of Education

William H. Schubert
Ming Fang He

In this book series, we explore panoramic landscapes of education. We invite a wide array of authors from diverse theoretical traditions and geographical locations around the world to ponder deeply and critically undulating and evolving contours of educational experience. We perceive contours of educational experience as landscapes that cultivate and are cultivated by who we were and how we become who we are as individuals and as humanity (Nussbaum, 1997). We engage with complex hills and rift valleys, rocky roads and serene pathways, war torn terrains and flowering gardens, towering trees and wuthering grasses, jagged cliffs and unyielding rocks, flowing rivers and uneven oceans evolving with flows of life that shape our perspectives, modify our ideas, and forge our actions. Building upon John Dewey's (1916) *democratic conception of education* and William Schubert's (2009) *ideals of love, justice, and education,* we perceive landscapes of education not only as schools but also as *gathering places* (Dewey, 1933) for humans to pursue worthwhile living. We honor the poetics of landscapes of education flourishing with divergence, convergence, diversity, and complexity of experience.

We look for authors who can move in new directions. We open dialogue on educational issues and situations of shared concerns. We create a space

Multiliteracies: Beyond Text and the Written Word, pages ix–xiii for educational workers such as public intellectuals, scholars, artists, and practitioners to engage in inquiries into education drawn from multiple perspectives such as art, music, language, literature, philosophy, history, social sciences, and professional studies. We welcome cross-disciplinary, interdisciplinary, trans-disciplinary, and counter-disciplinary work. We look for possibilities that are fresh and poetic, nuanced and novelistic, theoretical and practical, personal and political, imaginative and improvisational.

We expand parameters of educational inquiry substantively and methodologically. Substantively, books in this series explore multifarious landscapes wherever education occurs. Such explorations provocatively portray education in schools, workplaces, nonschool settings, and relationships. Methodologically, we encourage diverse forms of inquiry drawing on a wide array of research traditions, approaches, methods, and techniques such as ethnomethodology, phenomenology, hermeneutics, feminism, rhizomatics, deconstructionism, grounded theory, case studies, survey studies, interviews, participant observation, action research, teacher research, activist feminist inquiry, self study, life history, teacher lore, autobiography, biography, memoir, documentary studies, art-based inquiry, ethnography/critical ethnography, autoethnography, participatory inquiry, narrative inquiry, fiction, cross-cultural and multicultural narrative inquiry, psychoanalysis, queer inquiry, and personal~passionate~participatory inquiry.

We also feature works that amplify the educational value of mass media such as movies, DVDs, television, the Internet, comics, news comedy, cell phones, My Space and Face Book, videos, videogames, computers, and the World Wide Web. We hope to explore how we learn through such electronic frontiers in vastly new ways with little tutelage. We hope to encourage creative improvising, problem posing, critical inquiring, and joyful learning illuminated in these new ways of learning though electronic frontiers which are often suppressed and repressed in schooling. We hope to acknowledge the power of human beings to learn without lesson plans, manuals, worksheets, standardized tests, acquisitive rewards, or external standards.

We encourage expansions that move beyond Western orthodoxies to embrace landscapes from the Eastern (Asian), Southern (African and Latin American), and Oceanic (islandic) worlds. We especially want to see renditions move into *third spaces* (Gutiérrez, Rymes, & Larson, 1995) and *in-between* (He, 2003, 2010) that push boundaries, shift borders, dissolve barriers, and thrive upon contradictions of life. It is our intention that the works featured in this series reveal more of the world-wide landscapes of cultures, ideas, and practices that transgress dominant Western ideologies and their corporate and colonizing legacies. These works have potential in developing transcendent theories of decolonization (e.g., Tuhiwai Smith, 2001), advocating the liberty of indigenous language, cultural rights, and intellectualism (e.g., Grande, 2004), shattering *monocultures of the mind* (Shiva, 1993), overcoming perils of globalization, and inventing a better human condition for all.

We also highlight activist and social justice oriented research (e.g., Ayers, Quinn, & Stovall, 2009) and personal~passionate~participatory inquiry (e.g., He & Phillion, 2008) that engage participation of all citizens, encourage respect, innovation, interaction, cohesion, justice, and peace, and promote cultural, linguistic, intellectual, and ecological diversity and complexity. We celebrate postcolonial feminist work (e.g., Minh-ha, 1989; Mohanty, 2003/2005; Narayan, 1997) that explores migration, slavery, suppression, resistance, representation, difference, race, gender, place and responses to influential discourses of racism, sexism, classism, and colonialism. We also feature ecofeminist inquiry that explores the intersectionality of repatriarchal historical analysis, spirituality, racism, classism, imperialism, heterosexism, ageism, ableism, anthropocentrism, speciesism, and other forms of oppression (Mies & Shiva, 1993).

Books in this series focus on the what, why, how, when, where, and for whom of relationships, interactions, and transactions that transform human beings to different levels of awareness to build communities and public spaces with shared interests and common goals to strive for equitable, just, and invigorating human conditions. We seek explorations of the educational aspects of relationships (e.g., family, friendship), international, transnational, or intercultural understanding (e.g., exile, diaspora, displacement, indigenous knowledge), and circumstances of living (e.g., poverty, racism, alienation, war, colonization, oppression, and globalization). We want to see how languages, literacies, communities, homes, and families shape images of life's *mysteries and events* (Ulich, 1955), such as love, tradition, birth, death, success or failure, hopes of salvation, or immortality. These educational dimensions of life dynamically influence and are influenced by life in and out of schools (Schubert, 2010) and in-between (He, 2003, 2010). Through engaging such pursuits, this book series illuminates how human beings improvise lives (Bateson, 1989) and commitments in diverse, complicated, and often contested landscapes of education.

Unlike more definitively crafted book series that explicate inclusions and exclusions with ease and precision, our invitations continuously expand. The depths and breadths of landscapes where we live surpass everyday gaze and complicate static analysis. We showcase books that bring a sense of wonder and surprise, make the strange familiar and the familiar strange, and evoke what we do not expect. We do not narrow or define the topics of this series. Rather, we open doors to new perspectives, diverse paradigms, and creative possibilities. We invite authors to surprise us with their insightful ideas of what has been, what is, and what might be. For this volume, Eugene F. Provenzo, Jr., Amanda Goodwin, Miriam Lipsky, and Sheree Sharpe have surprised us with an inspiring compilation of explorations on *multiliteracies beyond text and the written words.*

References

Ayers, W., Quinn, T., & Stovall, D. (Eds.) (2009). *Handbook of social justice in education.* New York: Routledge.

Bateson, M. C. (1989). *Composing a life.* New York: The Atlantic Monthly Press.

Dewey, J. (1916). *Democracy and education.* New York: Macmillan.

Dewey, J. (1933). Dewey outlines utopian schools. *New York Times,* April 23, p 7. Also in Boydston, J. A. (Ed.), *The later works (1925–1953) of John Dewey,* Volume 9, (pp. 136–140) Carbondale, IL: Southern Illinois University Press, 1989.

Grande, S. (2004). *Red pedagogy: Native American social and political thought.* New York: Rowman & Littlefield.

Gutiérrez, K. D., Rymes, B., & Larson, J. (1995). Script, counterscript, and underlife in the classroom: James Brown versus Brown v. Board of Education. *Harvard Educational Review, 65*(3), 445–471.

He, M. F. (2003). *A river forever flowing: Cross-cultural lives and identities in the multicultural landscape.* Greenwich, CT: Information Age Publishers.

He, M. F. (2010). Exile pedagogy: Teaching in-between. In J. A. Sandlin, B. D. Schultz, & J. Burdick (Eds.), *Handbook of public pedagogy* (pp. 469–482). New York: Routledge.

He, M. F. & Phillion, J. (2008). *Personal~passionate~participatory inquiry into social justice in education.* Charlotte, NC: Information Age Publishing.

Mies, M., & Shiva, S. (1993). *Ecofeminism.* Halifax, Nova Scotia, Canada: Fernwood.

Minh-Ha, T. T. (1989). *Woman, native, other: Writing postcoloniality and feminism* (Midland Books). Bloomington, IN: Indiana University Press.

Mohanty, C. T. (2003/2005). *Feminism without borders: Decolonizing theory, practicing solidarity.* Durham, NC: Duke University Press.

Narayan, U. (1997). *Dislocating cultures: Identities, traditions, and third world feminism.* New York: Routledge.

Nussbaum, M. (1997). *Cultivating humanity: A classical defense of reform in liberal education.* Cambridge, MA: Harvard University Press.

Schubert, W. H. (2009). *Love, justice, and education: John Dewey and the Utopians.* Charlotte, NC: Information Age Publishing.

Schubert, W. H. (2010). Outside curriculum. In C. Kridel (Ed.), *Encyclopedia of curriculum studies* (pp. 624–628). Thousand Oaks, CA: Sage.

Shiva, V. (1993). *Monocultures of the mind: Perspectives on biodiversity and biotechnology.* Atlantic Highlands, NJ: Zed Books.

Tuhiwai Smith, L. (2001). *Decolonizing methodologies: Research and indigenous peoples.* London: Zed Books.

Ulich, R. (1955). Response to Ralph Harper's essay. In N. B. Henry. (Ed.), *Modern philosophies of education,* Fifty-fourth Yearbook (Part I) of the National Society for the Study of Education (pp. 254–257). Chicago: University of Chicago Press.

Preface

This is a book about literacy. It emphasizes literacies that are, or have been, common in American culture, but which tend to be ignored in more traditional discussions of literacy—specifically textual literacy.

Our approach in this book is experimental and deliberately playful. By describing *Multiliteracies* or *Alternative Literacies,* and how they function, we hope to develop a broader understanding of what it means to be literate in American culture. The writing of this book is a demonstration of the new literacy.

This book was researched and crafted as a shared and collective experience. Under the leadership of Professor Eugene F. Provenzo, Jr. in the Department of Teaching Learning, School of Education, University of Miami, a doctoral seminar titled Language, Literacy and Cultural Policy (TAL 723) was conducted in the spring of 2007 with seven graduate students: William Deese, Kathryn LeRoy, Wensen Lin, Maribel Harder, Yvonne Perry, Gabriel Quintana, and Lisa Repaskey. The course's instructor proposed that instead of writing traditional seminar papers, the members of the class would undertake a shared writing project for the semester—one that would lead to the creation of a collectively written book. The project was continued the following semester in a second course, Social and Cultural Foundations of Education (TAL 753). The members of this group extended and further developed the project. The four students in this second group were Jennifer Diptee, Amanda Goodwin, Miriam Lipsky, and Sheree Sharpe. Together with Provenzo, these students contributed their own essays, shot photos,

Multiliteracies: Beyond Text and the Written Word, pages xv–xvii and collected images, as well as taking on the task of being editors. Extra editorial work and effort were provided by Amanda Goodwin and Miriam Lipsy in the final stages of completing the project. Their efforts made the completion of this book possible.

We were assisted by Asterie Baker Provenzo in terms of editorial help. Her care and attention to detail have made this book a better final product.

In doing so, we consciously engaged in an act of "collective intelligence" or "cosmopedic" process through the creation of a "textual community." We were aided in this process by the use of online technology in the specific form of a wiki, as well as electronic mail and online posting systems.[1] With the help of Bill Vilberg at the University of Miami's Instructional Advancement Center, a wiki was set up for the course. Between the two groups, a list was identified of approximately seventy-five Multi or Alternative Literacies. Those considered most interesting were selected for the individual chapters included in this work.

In undertaking this book, we asked the question fundamental to this series, which is: How is the experience of students changing outside of the experience of school, and how do those changes potentially shape the work they do, how they learn, and the lives they lead in schools?

Our postmodern culture clearly demands and reflects new literacies. These new literacies not only affect the general population, but also the students in our educational system. Our increasing diversity, and recognition of difference, brings with it demands for a broader understanding of what it means to be literate. Multiliteracy becomes a necessity.

On a final note, we believe that this work reflects both traditional literacies and new models of research. This is a book about literacies and about traditional and popular culture. Throughout this book we have drawn heavily on visual sources from the shared photo site *Flickr.* We feel that the use of these materials is very much in the spirit of the Alternative and Multi-literacies that are the subject of this book. In much the same spirit, we have decided to break with academic tradition and reference throughout our essays the online encyclopedia *Wikipedia.* We do so in recognition that it reflects the emerging culture of literacy in ways that are not always captured by traditional research sources. While we do not always consider *Wikipedia* an authoritative source, we do believe it to be both a useful and often helpful source.

—Eugene F. Provenzo, Jr.
University of Miami
Winter 2010

Note

1. For those not familiar with it, a wiki is a piece of computer software that allows a user to create and edit web page content using a web browser. Essentially it is an Internet device that makes it possible to have a group of people write and edit on a project with one another. The first wiki site was created for the Portland Pattern Repository in 1995. Its most well-known use is in the form of the encyclopedia project known as *Wikipedia*, whose English edition, as of February 2007, included 2,322,704 articles.

Introduction

Literacy for the 21st Century

According to the Oxford English Dictionary, literacy is defined as "The quality or state of being literate; knowledge of letters; condition in respect to education, esp. ability to read and write" (Literate, 1989). This definition probably fits a model most people think of when they hear the word literacy. It does not, however, take into account the many different literacies that are evident in our culture and day-to-day lives. Many of these literacies are taken for granted. Some are very new. Some are quite old.

For example, oral literacy predates textual literacy, yet oral literacy is rapidly emerging in our culture in new forms—a process that began in the late 19th century. Starting with the telephone in the 1880s and 1890s, we have moved increasingly towards the use of new forms of oral communication aided through technological innovations. In addition, these technical innovations have made possible multimodal means of communication such as e-mail, text messaging, and instant messaging. Harvey J. Graff (1995), perhaps the most well-known scholar interested in the history of literacy, explains some of these modalities as:

> many literacies in addition to or "beyond" "traditional" alphabet literacy—from those of science and numeracy, to the spatial literacy that some geographers term "graphicacy", to the loudly touted and seemingly highly vulnerable "cultural literacy", "historical literacy", and "moral literacy". Some among the lengthening lists are long established in presumption but much more novel discursively or semantically: ecological literacy, "teleliteracy" and other media literacies, food literacy, emotional literacy, sexual literacy. (p. 321)

Multiliteracies: Beyond Text and the Written Word, pages xix–xxv

These "many literacies" or multiliteracies—a term coined by a group of literacy scholars from the United States, Great Britain, and Australia called the New London Group (1996)—rest on the belief that literacy is socially constructed and dynamic in nature. According to the New London Group, mulitiliteracies have emerged as a result of new communications and an increasingly global culture in which cultural and linguistic diversity is more and more the norm.

Multiliteracies go beyond traditional textual models of literacy by focusing on "modes of representation much broader than language alone. These differ according to culture and context, and have specific cognitive, cultural, and social effects" (The New London Group, 1996, p. 64). Thus, "In some cultural contexts—in an Aboriginal community or in a multimedia environment, for instance—the visual mode of representation may be much more powerful and closely related to language than 'mere literacy' would ever be able to allow" (The New London Group, 1996, p.4).

Keeping the multiliteracy perspective of the New London Group in mind, this book attempts to map the literacies than can be found in contemporary culture. Something like this has been done in Colin Lankshear and Michael Knobel's *A New Literacies Sampler*. While we feel that their work is useful from a theoretical point of view, we try in this collection to go beyond what they have done by providing further examples of multiliteracies at work. Our approach is exploratory and descriptive. We recognize that it is unavoidably incomplete. Our purpose has been to identify multiliteracies and then attempt to define how they operate and function. Ultimately, we are interested in the question of what is literacy in a postmodern, post-typographic and global culture.

We have debated using the term "alternative literacies" instead of multiliteracies to categorize the phenomenon we are interested in. We have abandoned the term, at least in our title, deliberating linking our exploration to the work of the New London Group. Organizing our essays has been a challenge. Multiliteracies, by definition, represent a complex phenomenon. They can be both old and new. Emoticons—symbols created with a typing keyboard used to convey emotions—are part of the new multiliteracies while recalling an earlier form—hieroglyphics. Similarly, roadside memorials—memorials created for people killed in auto crashes—hearken back to Mexican and Hispanic burial traditions.

Other multiliteracies are unique to our era—what we would describe as distinctly postmodern. These include the Human Genome Project, which precisely maps the genetic code of human beings. Another example would be the AIDS Memorial Quilt, which was a social response to the AIDS epidemic that emerged in the 1980s. In a certain sense, its representation of the AIDS crisis represents a unique cultural expression—a distinct literate communication—its size taking up many football fields in length and width, its creation national, if not global. And yet, in the end the AIDS quilt echoed and employed previous literate forms—that is, quilting as a communal and literate act.

Like the New London Group, while we do not want to downplay the significance of reading and writing to the process of human communication and literacy, we believe that limiting our notions of literacy to reading and writing does not fit with the reality of human experience, nor does it encompass increasingly complex postmodern realities. Not to include multiliteracies in our understanding of literacy limits our ability to comprehend what is actual human literacy—that is, as it manifests itself in our daily social, political, and cultural systems.

Unlike traditional textual literacy, alternative literacy is often more democratic and inclusive. Expert knowledge is not limited to people who have mastered traditional methods and skills of reading and writing. Thus with rap music, a particularly effective artist may not necessarily be literate in the traditional textual sense, but may be more advanced in poetic forms, lyrical composition, and socio-cultural expression that is the essence of the rapper's art.

Multiliteracies also operate within the social and cultural realm. Thus the meaning of numbers and colors may be significant in various ways across different cultures. In western culture, white is associated with purity and innocence, whereas in Chinese, culture white is associated with death and mourning. Similarly, the use of numbers across cultures can imply very different ways of knowing and understanding the world. The number 666 in Chinese culture implies the idea of things "going smoothly" and "good luck." In western culture, on the contrary, 666 refers to the "Mark of the Beast" or the Antichrist.

By defining the highest level of literacy in Western Culture as being almost exclusively based in reading or writing, we tend to discount the importance of other forms of literacy—literacies that can provide us different and potentially deeper insights and experiences than simply the use of traditional textual forms. Thus, for example, the oral tradition of story telling takes the Western textual tradition of the author as authority, and recreates storytelling as a collective and shared experience. As part of the bardic tradition of poetry in Ancient Greece, figures such as Homer were not one author, but many authors. As a result the story-telling process became not only a shared collective experience, but a system of shared insight, wisdom, and intelligence—one in which many authors contribute to a single narrative.

In this context, Olson (2001), drawing on the works of Coulmas (1989) and DeFrancis (1989) argues that: "the traditional assumption that the history of writing is the progressive evolution that culminates in the alphabet is misleading in the ethnocentrism implicit in such a view" (p. 110). Multiliteracies, and more specifically alternative literacies, by their very existence recognize other ways of viewing the world. As such, they are potentially volatile and dangerous as compared to more traditional forms.

Why is this the case? With rap music, individuals who otherwise have little power or authority in the culture are able to express injustices, criticize privilege, resist mainstream norms, raise social consciousness, and pose alternative ways of viewing the world. "Normative" is challenged through critique and alternative ways of knowing.

Like rap music, graffiti or "tagging" allows individuals whose voices are not typically heard in the public arena the opportunity to express themselves and "make meaning" about the events in their lives. This involves a "dialectic process," in which, according to Arnove and Graff (2001), there is "an interaction between individuals and the environment as they gain literacy, and between them and centralizing authorities" (p. 615).

In the case of graffiti and tagging, this is quite literally the process that is at work, as the individual leaves his mark in communities where he or she would normally be largely invisible. In this context, graffiti and tagging need to be understood "not simply an act of vandalism or violence; it is a social practice with its own rules and codes—a literacy practice imbued with intent and meaning" (MacGillivray & Curwen, 2007, p. 354). Graffiti and tagging of course raise important questions about what is "appropriate." Is tagging a public wall simply a use of a public space? What if only part of the community wants the wall tagged? This was a major problem with the work of graffiti artists during the 1960s and 1970s in places such as New York City. A spray painted and tagged subway or rail car is one person's art and another person's vandalism. Legal issues involving personal and communal property rights emerge. It is worth noting, for example, that in the forty or fifty years since graffiti was first introduced that it has come to be increasingly accepted—now beginning to even be part of mainstream art commoditized by galleries and exhibited by museums. Nonetheless, many people maintain that expressing oneself through graffiti in a public space is a violation of the "commons"—one involving the forcing of one person's aesthetic or literacy on another.

Too closely identifying multiliteracies with certain groups such as African Americans can have the potential to misrepresent their literacy. While we believe that rap, for example, is an important part of African-American literacy, it does not primarily define African Americans. McHenry and Heath (2001) argue that by primarily focusing on expressions of oral literacy such as rap music, other forms that have been historically important are ignored: "African Americans, through many of the very forms most closely associated with 'oral' features, have based their communication to a great extent on writing and reading" (p. 273).

Why, then, are alternative literacies important? We believe, and try to demonstrate in this work, that they are important because they often empower people to act and be heard in the world in ways that they are not otherwise able to do. In this context, they are literally enabled through the literacy process that is distinctively cultural and often exclusively their subgroup's possession. In this context, according to Paulo Freire (2001), literacy is a deeply cultural and political act—one that is potentially oppositional. It is more than "memorizing sentences, words, or syllables—lifeless objects unconnected to an existential universe—but rather an attitude of creation and re-creation, a self-transformation producing a stance of intervention in one's context." (p. 622)

Other alternative literacies raise social consciousness in ways that are different from rap music. Hmong story cloths—embroidered cloths with narrative stories created by Hmong refugees from the mountain regions of Cambodia, Vietnam, and Thailand—express cultural history (exile, war, and day-to-day life), while sharing the collective experience of the Hmong people with not only themselves, but a worldwide audience.

As mentioned earlier, many of the multiliteracies that have emerged in recent years have been dependent on technological developments. Instant messaging—where people communicate via typed text in real time—is such an example. Assuming that instant messaging is indeed useful to people, we can see how technology is beneficial, confirming Walter Ong's (2001) argument that "Technology properly interiorized does not degrade human life, but on the contrary enhances it" (p. 24). Modalities such as text messaging and social networking sites such as Facebook significantly expand the communication options of many people. Rarely does one walk through a crowded street or college campus without seeing people sending text messages by means of their cell phones or Blackberries.

For some groups, such as the deaf, a technology like text messaging represents a means of empowerment by expanding their capacity to communicate. Multi and alternative literacies can empower groups who would otherwise be excluded or marginalized in the mainstream culture. With developments in technology such as text messaging—real-time communication with text via one's cell phone or other hand-held electronic device—one sees the quality of human life enriched for deaf and hard-of-hearing youth and young adults. They can create communities and networks of communication with other deaf and hard-of-hearing individuals or with non-hearing-impaired individuals in ways that were not previously possible.

Other proactive uses of text messaging that represent multi and alternative literacies include helpful reminders "texted" to college students in treatment programs struggling with issues such as smoking and bulimia—thus serving as an aid in freeing these young adults from unhealthy addictions and behaviors. In doing so, they can be actively linked to support groups in real time in ways that would not necessarily be possible without the use of technology. As a consequence, "the use of technology can enrich the human psyche, enlarge human spirit, set it free, intensify its interior life." (Ong, 2001, p. 24).

* * *

What is the relevance or importance of multi and alternative literacies to practitioners in the field of education? We believe that they are important because they represent a means by which learners can be culturally and politically empowered. Through these literacies, other points of view and perspectives are brought into play. In addition, individuals are provided with multiple avenues to express themselves and means by which to interpret the world around them.

Multi and alternative literacies can enhance traditional forms of reading and writing by providing a richer environment in which text and writing can be situated. In doing so, they can make traditional reading and writing a more authentic experience for the learner. Thus students using instant messaging, emoticons, and other alternative literacies in textual communication are, in fact, potentially reinforcing textual forms and writing as a means of communication, while employing new modalities.

This leads us to the paradoxical situation that as students become seemingly less literate in terms of traditional models of literacy, they may, in fact, be building traditional literacy skills—that is, reading and writing through the use of multiliteracies.

What is clear, as the essays in this book demonstrate, is that literacy in our culture is fluid and changing, and much more complex than is typically perceived. Teachers in the classroom must be aware and sensitive to the multiform and complex literacies that are at work around them, and how they contribute to the identity of their students, their diversity, and the multiple ways they communicate in the classroom and their day-to-day worlds.

They also need to help students "read the world" in new ways from the Human Genome Project to body language or interpersonal intelligence. In doing so, literacy and its definition will be expanded beyond text and writing to include a wider range of human experience—it will more clearly represent the reality of what literacy actually is and how it functions in our culture.

1

Hypertext

An Interactive Literacy

Eugene F. Provenzo, Jr.
Amanda P. Goodwin

Examples of hypertext on the White House website. Photograph by Amanda Goodwin.

Multiliteracies: Beyond Text and the Written Word, pages 1–5

Hypertext is a multiliteracy that has changed the way we read. Ted Nelson (1987) defines it as "*non-sequential writing*—text that allows choice to the reader, best read as an interactive screen" (p. 0/2). The literary scholar and art historian George Landow (1989) explains that in the case of hypertext, "The defining characteristics of this new information medium derive from its combination of blocks of text joined by electronic links, for this combination emphasizes multiple connections rather than linear reading or organization" (p. 39). Jeff Conklin (1987) describes hypertext as a system which makes possible "direct machine-supported references from one textual chunk to another; new interfaces provide the user with the ability to interact directly with these chunks and to establish new relationships between them" (p. 17).

Providing multiple meanings through different styles of text or footnotes is by no means a new phenomenon. Italic typefaces, which have their origins in the Renaissance, have a hypertext function by linking us to secondary meanings such as the title of a book, the use of a foreign word, or a *special emphasis*. Similarly, in addition to crediting sources, footnotes expand meaning by establishing a link to another body of literature making possible a discussion at a secondary level—one that functions beneath the main current of the text.

Footnote = Link = Primitive Hypertext

The problem with footnotes of course is that the sources they refer to are rarely immediately accessible. You are reading a useful source, but the library is closed, or the book is checked out and so on. If a source is important enough, you eventually track it down. Often the result is that the work cited was not that informative or useful—often not worth the wait or delay it caused in developing a line of thought. The beauty of a well-developed hypertext system is that the sources are instantly available in a useable format to the reader. In addition, the reader can, depending on his or her interests and sophistication, delve into the text at different levels of interpretation and complexity.

In the following example of the Aesopic Fable, "In Unity is Strength," hypertext links, indicated by the boxed areas below, provide a second level of meaning for the text. In doing so, the reader is able to establish complex "links" between the text and larger domains of information.

Michael Joyce (1995) argues that hypertext, which he equates with hypermedia, is first and foremost a visual form, which embodies information and communications, artistic and affective constructs, and conceptual ab-

IN UNITY IS STRENGTH: THE BUNDLE OF STICKS

An old man on the point of death summoned his sons round him to give them some parting advice. He ordered his servants to bring in a faggot of sticks and said to his eldest son: "Break it" The son strained and strained, but with all his efforts was unable to break the Bundle. The other sons also tried, but none of them were successful. "Untie the faggots," said the father, "and each of you take a stick." When they had done so, he called out to them: "Now break," and each stick was easily broken. "You see my meaning," said their father.

"A Union gives strength."

The source of this text is: Joseph Jacobs, *The Fables of Aesop*, illustrated by Richard Heighway, first published in 1894, p. 174.

Fasces, which can be seen at the bottom of the illustration, were a faggot of sticks or **wooden** **rods** that were fastened around an **axe** and held together with a leather strap. *Fasces* were a symbol of the authority and power of the Roman republic and were carried by Roman judges as a symbol of authority. Their origin can be traced back to the fable of *The Old Man and the Bundle of Sticks*. *Fasces* provide the origin for the modern term facist. *Fasces* were often incorporated into Nazi propaganda and symbols.

In a hypertext or hypermedia system, every reference can be linked to a secondary data source, whether an illustration, further text, a film clip or sound file.

stracts alike into symbolic structures made visible on a computer-controlled display. It is a form, according to Joyce, in which print gives way to digitized sound, animation, video, virtual reality, and computer networks or databases that are linked to it. Images can be "read" as though they are texts. In all of this, the computer and linked networked systems are key, whether on a closed system such as a free standing computer, or a machine linked to the global infrastructure of the Internet and World Wide Web. It is the computer, and its active screen, that transforms hypertext into a new form of literacy. How is hypertext different than traditional text? How does it change the nature of reading?

Unlike linear text, which is typically read from top to bottom and left to right, hypertext is multilinear, with no exact start or finish (Spires & Estes, 2001). Hypertext works in an associative manner, connecting related ideas through hyperlinks (Provenzo, in press). Hypertext comprehension involves understanding this dynamic, three-dimensional text and the processes of exploration and processing that is demanded from such tasks. When reading online, the reader may choose to link to different websites or supporting topics. The reader is active. He or she must choose which link to explore next and at what point to end the reading process.

Hypertext and traditional texts differ in who designs the path of reading. For example, authors of traditional text establish the pattern of reading, whereas hypertext allows the reader to choose his or her own path among topics and subtopics. While this interaction with hypertext empowers the reader, researchers admit "the freedom of choice and interest that drives the reading process in hypertext can become diverted by potential cognitive overload" (Spires & Estes, 2001). To control the large and potentially overwhelming amount of material available on the web, options such as Webquests give readers a more definitive path through hypertexts.

The demands of reading hypertext are much greater than those of reading traditional text. Hypertext requires readers to activate reading strategies in order to choose the path of the text. When reading a document on the Internet, readers must be able to navigate across multiple screens or windows, using parallel processing, pattern recognition, and strategic thinking. In developing fluency in reading hypertext, readers must become active. Reading in a hypertext environment potentially shapes reading in more traditional print/paper environments. It is reasonable to assume that readers experienced with a hypertext environment are more likely to search for supporting materials, and to see reading as less of a continuous process, but instead as something that comes in "chunks" or "bits."

In addition, the ability to read hypertext is somewhat dependent on the skills of the reader in manipulating technology. As these skills increase, the efficiency of reading hypertext improves as well. Knowledge of simple tricks can improve the ease of accessing hypertext. For example, PC users can open multiple windows and move between them by pressing alt + tab, and Mac users can view all windows and choose among them by scrolling to the bottom of the screen and using the window view. Efficiency with search engines such as Google is also important in helping to find and limit the vast information sources available on the Internet. Using quotation marks to link words in your search can help readers find information more pertinent to their interests. The development of online bookmarks or "favorites" provides organized storage for sites that have been visited and are deemed useful (Provenzo, in press).

Hypertext offers readers instantaneous access to huge quantities of text and graphics. This multiliteracy connects online texts by linking similar ideas through hyperlinks. Traditional literacy involves reading texts where further information on a topic, definitions of challenging words, and details about related topics exist in separate books or texts that readers have to physically retrieve before being able to connect the information into an overall picture. Hypertext makes the above connections available immediately. As students become more practiced in reading hypertext, they bring such concepts of association, integration, and interaction to traditional literacy as well.

2

Facebook and Social Networking Sites

The Multiliteracy of Personal and Professional Network Building

Amanda P. Goodwin

A Facebook user going to her homepage. Photograph by Eugene F. Provenzo, Jr.

Multiliteracies: Beyond Text and the Written Word, pages 7–11

Along with new technologies, literacy is evolving. Facebook.com and other social networking websites have created a new multliteracy connecting people and sharing information through social graphs, which are "digital mappings of people's real-world social connections" (Facebook, 2008). With over 50 million users, half of whom return daily, Facebook changes traditional static text into a more interactive, changing, and far-reaching form (Facebook, 2008). Within minutes, users can create a profile and send out requests for acquaintances to become "friends." They can take advantage of Facebook's networks to connect to old friends as well as create new relationships. Because these networks include affiliations to colleges, high schools, local associations, activity groups, and more, users receive "friend" requests from people associated with many different parts of their lives, including friends lost for many years.

Unlike traditional literacy, in which authors create and readers interpret meaning from fixed text, Facebook introduces users to a new interactive medium that requires them to interact and respond to text, as well as become authors of their own texts. In addition to changing the nature of text interaction, the multiliteracy of Facebooking eliminates distance between users by providing instantaneous communication among clients throughout the world. Beyond flirting, corresponding, and interacting, Facebook creates a process that makes it possible for online users to link multiple networks of people in a virtual social web.

Started by Mark Zuckerman in 2004 when he was a student at Harvard University, Facebook was originally designed as an online version of paper photo albums that helped students connect a name with a face—crudely known in the 1960s as "Pigbooks." As the website grew, Facebook evolved into a more student friendly version of other social networking sites such as Friendster and MySpace.

From its start, Facebook was extremely popular. Within its first week of existence, almost 1,000 Harvard students joined (Reed, 2004). When access to Facebook was expanded to include all Ivy League colleges and some other institutions including Stanford University, the University of Chicago, and the University of Virginia, the number of users increased to 120,000 (Reed, 2004). As a result of the popularity of Facebook, the company further expanded access to the general public in September of 2006 (Facebook, 2008). Facebook now has users in multiple countries. In fact, in November of 2007, with Facebook valued at approximately $15 billion dollars, Microsoft and two equity capital firms invested $750 million in the company (Abram, 2008).

Section of a Facebook page showing the overlap of friends and different personal associations by network. Photograph by Amanda Goodwin.

With all this success, Facebook has created a new means of communication and interaction. When users log onto the site, they can view mini-feeds that inform the user of friend updates. The user can also view updates on friends found on their profile pages. One of the most innovative features of Facebook is the ability to use the networks and friends of friends to meet new people or rekindle lost relationships. The number of ways to meet people on Facebook seems endless. For example, by clicking on a friend's profile, a user can view all the friends of that friend. If the user wants to become "friends" with that person, then the user can click on a symbol to send a request to become that person's "friend." The user can also view the networks of friends, and through that medium, access a whole new set of people to meet or become reacquainted with. Another way of meeting people is through the "groups" application, which shows networks and groups that have been joined by current friends. Users can also find other users in their geographical area who share similar interests.

Facebook features allow for more than just meeting and reading about friends. Facebook user pages provide information on a user's status of being single, in a relationship, or married. As a result, users can search through

A Facebook user's profile includes relationship status. Photograph by Amanda Goodwin.

friends of friends, networks, or people with similar interests for potential dates. Because such potential dates have something in common, initiating the dating process is less intimidating. "The principle behind the popularity of [Facebook] is simple: The networks make meeting people seem like a casual process" (Reed, 2004, p. A30).

Facebook also encourages interaction among users. In addition to searching for and adding "friends," users can email, send a gift, send a poke, add a comment to the person's wall (which is similar to a message board), and choose from many applications. Facebook also links users to a common online marketplace where users can post jobs, rental properties, real estate, goods, free stuff, and so forth. Another option provided by Facebook is the event calendar that informs users of personal and friends' events.

Facebook is not just used for personal reasons. Businesses and educational institutions have created pages as a way of reaching out to targeted groups of people. In fact, schools, libraries, volunteer organizations, major league sports teams, political candidates, political parties, and even governmental organizations have pages. In terms of the 2008 Presidential Election, Barack Obama has a personal page and three organizational pages dedicated to his run for presidency. Hilary Clinton also has her own personal page and an organizational page. Similarly, John McCain has a personal page and two organizational pages. In terms of recruiting, business schools like the University of Toronto's Rotman School of Management in Ontario, Canada even created an admissions page, which attracted 158 members within a few months. According to the Assistant Dean and Executive Director of MBA programs, "[Facebook] enables us to talk to candidates whom we are unable to reach through traditional methods" (Powers, 2008, p. 64).

Facebook provides users with innovative applications and a myriad of possibilities to use for both personal and professional reasons. Because of this, users must learn the unique multiliteracy that is associated with communicating on Facebook. Unlike traditional literacy that uses standard paper and text, the mulitliteracy created by Facebook requires users to communicate in an online form through text, applications, and pictorial symbols. To take full advantage of Facebook's many applications, users must become familiar with the structure of Facebook. For example, each user's profile page has a picture of the user on the top left, a link to friends' pages on the middle left, a list of networks and number of friends in each network on the bottom left of the page, updates about friends on the middle right, and so on. Etiquette, safety, and tone of messages on Facebook must also be learned. Schools are now beginning to teach such lessons to students. With 55% of 12–17 year olds reporting that they belong to social networking sites such as Facebook, teachers are instructing students on how to safely use the tools of Facebook (O'Hanlon, 2007). Facebook has even gained such popularity that it is now a commonly used verb.

In conclusion, Facebook represents a social networking site that has created a unique multiliteracy, which is spoken at various levels of expertise by millions of people. In many ways it recalls aspects of earlier human cultural associations and configurations such as tribalism, while doing so with the most contemporary of technologies.

3

Environmental Print

Lisa Repaskey

Starbucks as an example of environmental print. Photograph by Lisa Repaskey.

Multiliteracies: Beyond Text and the Written Word, pages 13–15

We are bombarded by print everywhere we look. Strings of letters and numbers fill street signs, billboards, freeway signs, signs on buildings, clothing, TV shows, newspapers, books, store signs, fast food, boxes, wrappers, news channels, and graffiti, just to name a few. The Literacy Dictionary (1995) refers to all of this as environmental print, which also includes road signs and handmade signs, such as advertising garage sales or a poster listing rules in an elementary school classroom. Commercially produced company and product logos, such as Starbucks, McDonalds, and Nike, which also constitute environmental print, are referred to in business terms as "branding" (Horner, 2005). According to Merriam-Webster.com, "branding" is a marketing term that refers to "the promoting of a product or service by identifying it with a particular brand" (Branding, 2004).

Environmental print is a key element that links the literate remnants of our literacy history to the present as we move from an oral tradition into one that is written. In ancient times, emblems such as seals, totem poles, coats of arms, hallmarks, banners, and religious signs represented types of graphic codes used (Gaur, 1984/1987). Presently, we still utilize graphic codes in what we consider as environmental print. Emblems are much like names because they represent things, not words.

As literate individuals, why is environmental print important? We can read the letters and numbers around us and make meaning out of them. Because of this, environmental print is an important first step into the world of literacy for young children. In the research of Duke and Purcell-Gates (2003), it is shown that, through everyday events in their homes and communities, young children are constantly learning about literacy and how print works by observing the enormous amount of print in all aspects of life and through observing adults' interaction with that print.

McDonalds' logo of the Golden Arches. Photograph by Lisa Repaskey.

When driving around town, it is a common occurrence for a child who sees the golden arches logo to exclaim, "McDonald's!" "Hamburger! French fries!" The relation of this symbol to meaning is a key preliteracy skill.

Unique company logos, such as the Nike "swoosh," Chuck E. Cheese with the mouse in the blue hat, Trix cereal with the "silly rabbit," Target with its trademark red circle inside another red circle, and of course, McDonald's with its huge golden arches provide instant recognition by the consumer. And it's in this recognition of specific logos that young children begin to explore details of print. Marie Clay (1993) found such explorations result in the development of print concepts, allowing them to create rudimentary hypotheses about the letters, words and message surrounding them (Clay 1993).

"Stop sign." Photograph by Lisa Repaskey.

Environmental print is more than just company logos. It also consists of street signs, like the STOP sign with its familiar red octagon, a railroad crossing with a black X and the letters "RR" on a yellow circle, highway exit signs printed in white with a green background, and billboards advertising just about everything imaginable. Environmental print extends itself to newspapers, books, and magazines found around the home, as well as cooking and cleaning supplies. It's also the No Smoking sign with a cigarette in a circle with a line through it, the stick figures of a man and a woman that indicates a public bathroom, and banners in store windows proclaiming sales.

Everywhere we look in our world, environmental print surrounds us. Whether it's the familiar corporate logo that provides an instantaneous connection between the brand and the product, or the numerous arrays of pictures that share specific information located within that particular picture or symbol, environmental print is a powerful type of alternative literacy.

4

The City as Text

Eugene F. Provenzo, Jr.

Times Square on a cloudy day. Photograph by Miriam Lipsky.

Multiliteracies: Beyond Text and the Written Word, pages 17–20

The nature of environmental print is rapidly changing. Nowhere is this clearer than in an environment such as Times Square in New York City—particularly at night. The idea of cities lit at night—ones that often include electrified signs—is taken for granted by most people. In fact, the idea of the city as an electrified space almost certainly dates back to the electrification of the Pan-American Exposition in Buffalo, New York in 1901.

Electrified signs were seen by the German Bauhaus Movement as redefining the nighttime space of cities—one that introduced text into the nighttime space—literally bringing the written word into spaces that had previously been dark, or at best, dimly illuminated by the gaslights of Victorian culture.

Text became dynamic in nighttime spaces with the introduction of neon light bulbs, which could be shaped into letters and programmed to flash on and off. Signs of this type became a common textual form in American cities—letting people know that there was a "Diner" or place where they could "Eat" and that it was open.

Las Vegas extended this idea of the city as text during the period following the Second World War by creating enormous animated signs that

Advertising a theatrical show—Lew Fields Herald Square Theatre (Broadway, New York City), 1908. Courtesy of the Library of Congress.

announced the availability of gambling and entertainment and broadcast the names of hotels such as the Luxor and Stardust.

These early examples of the electrification of text as part of cityscapes were modernist inventions—ones that were a direct outgrowth of industrialization. The creation of what was literally described as "A City of Light" at the Pan-American Exposition in Buffalo in 1901, for example, was a direct result of the massive electrification project that had just come online due to the generation of hydroelectric power from Niagara Falls.

Text in the form of data streaming illuminating the night can be seen with the news summaries posted by the New York *Times* in the 1930s around the side of their building on Herald Square in the Times Square area of New York City. The New York *Times* news "ticker" was a limited textual display—one that was transformed as a result of the development of computers and flat screen display systems in the last couple of decades. This transformation, which was anticipated in the "meditatrons" that were such a prominent element in the 1980 science fiction film *Bladerunner* , have become a reality in cities such as Tokyo, Shanghai, and New York City.

In New York City, for example, a six to seven block area centered around Times Square represents the type of radical text and visual space that was anticipated over twenty-five years ago in *Bladerunner.* Corporate logos are seen everywhere including logos for Bank America, Coca Cola, Samsung, McDonald's, Kodak, and Mars Candy (M & Ms). Signs, 100 by 20 feet, with flashing and moving text advertising "Wrestlemania" and similar events line the cityscape. Buildings and their architecture fade away as they are consumed—literally wrapped with messages whose neon signs are not simply in motion, but practically explode and encompass the sides of the buildings on which they are illuminated. Advertisements for musicals and current television programs as part of the "Bright lights of Broadway" dominate all that surrounds them.

Not only text and advertisements, but various forms of media dominate the area. Often they transmit images from television news headquarters that are located around Times Square such as ABC and NBC. Action on the street is projected onto the screens above for all to see—visitors to the Square become part of a spectacle in which they observe themselves included on the giant screens found on many of the buildings.

Similar scenes are to be found in other major urban centers. The scale is enormous as traditional text transforms itself into media graphics and other new forms of graphic representation. A new type of textuality, and in turn, a new literacy, is rapidly coming into being—one that is fluid and dynamic and that is becoming embedded in the businesses, entertainment

M & M World in Times Square. Photograph by Miriam Lipsky.

centers, and places where we live. Students who grow up in such environments take for granted these new and emerging forms of textuality. Schools must teach students to understand the link between print-based and image-based environments—a link that functions symbiotically. Through this type of knowledge, students gain a secondary level of literate understanding (Piro, 2002).

5

Emoticons

William B. Deese

Examples of ancient Egyptian hieroglyphic symbols.

Hieroglyphics, or writing that uses symbols rather than letters or words, have been used for thousands of years. Since the introduction of the Gutenberg press in the middle of the fifteenth century, written communication in Western culture has been dominated by textual or alphabetic forms. Recently, the introduction of the computer has renewed interest in and increased the use of hieroglyphic and communication symbols in writing. An example of this resurgence is emoticons.

Lara Rezabeck and John Cochenour (1995) define emoticons as "visual cues formed from ordinary typographical symbols that when read sideways represent feelings or emotions" (p. 1). Graphic emoticons, or small images that replace text are often used in conjunction with text messaging, instant messenger programs, and in Internet forums (Emoticons, 2006). Graphic emoticons return writing to the visual modalities found in early hieroglyphic forms. As such, they represent a significant shift in the type of literacy used in our culture.

:) = Typographic ☺ = Graphic

Multiliteracies: Beyond Text and the Written Word, pages 21–23

The origins of textual emoticons can be traced to the first part of the twentieth century. One of the earliest proposed uses began with the celebrated American author Ambrose Bierce (1842–1914), who proposed, "an improvement in punctuation—the snigger point, or note of cachinnation: it is written thus _/! And presents, as near may be, a smiling mouth. It is to be appended, with the full stop, [or exclamation mark as Bierce's later example used] to every jocular or ironical sentence" (Emoticons, 2006, p. 2).

A more recent example of early uses of emoticons occurred on September 19, 1982, when Scott Fahlman of Carnegie Mellon University proposed that the ASCII emoticons :-) and :-(be used to express emotion on a computer science general message board (Emoticons, 2006). The use of these symbols for this purpose has become widespread in the last twenty-five years.

Whereas textual emoticons were born in the early twentieth century, graphical emoticons first emerged in the mid twentieth century from the creative mind of freelance artist Harvey Ball, who in 1963 created the famous yellow "smiley face" for a large insurance company. This image is credited as the source of inspiration for many of the graphical emoticons used today (Emoticons, 2006).

The widespread use of emoticons in computer-mediated communication (CMC) began with the use of e-mail. Because of the limitations of written text in conveying emotional tone and nuance, emoticons have provided a means of adding a valuable dimension to e-mail messages. Written texts, such as e-mail, are devoid of nonverbal cues that provide a secondary level of meaning in face-to-face communication. Without this interpersonal information, e-mail users often rely upon emoticons to help convey the intended meaning of a written message (Rezabek & Cochenour, 1995). These emoticons, which are used to represent actual facial expressions, allow e-mailers to imbue their messages with social meaning (Walther & D'Addario, 2001), which better defines the intended message of the written text.

How effective are emoticons at conveying emotions? In a recent study that incorporated an MRI to measure brain activity, Yuasa, Saito, and Mukawa (2006), determined that when humans encounter emoticons, they

:)	Happy
: (	Sad
;)	Winking
:D	big grin

Examples of commonly used textually based emoticons.

detect the emotions of the writer even though they do not perceive the emoticons themselves as a face. In fact, when graphic emoticons are applied during online sales negotiations, they have measurable effects on the buyer's decision making.

As emoticons come into increasing use, their importance as a type of postmodern literacy increases as well. E-mail is now the most common form of computer-mediated communication, and for many, it is the most common form of overall communication other than the spoken word. It has also been proposed that e-mail, as a form of CMC, may eventually surpass face-to-face interactions (Walther & D'Addario, 2001).

As we become more dependent on e-mail as a form of communication, the use of emoticons increases. In Witmer and Katzman's study (1997), approximately 3,000 messages in Usenet newsgroup postings were analyzed for content, showing that over 13% of all messages contained emoticons. In a similar attempt to analyze the use of emoticons, Rezabeck and Cochenour (1995) examined four academic listserves, finding that emoticons existed in approximately 19% to 75% of messages.

Emoticons are a form of modern literacy that provide an emotional context to e-mail, text messaging, and other means of technological communication. Without the existence of emoticons, technology users are reliant upon a more limited form of literacy, one that is devoid of necessary emotional symbols. As Walther and D'Addario (2001) state, "It is clear that emoticons have become commonplace in computer mediated communication, and emoticons have obviously found their way into the lexicon of the computer-using world" (p. 327). They are clearly an important element in a new and emerging postmodern literacy.

6

Instant and Text Messaging

Maribel G. Harder

2NITE = Tonight	MorF = Male or Female
ADR = Address	MU = Miss You
ASL = Age/Sex/Location	OMG = Oh My God
B4YKI = Before You Know It	P911 = Parent Alert
BC = Because	PIR = Parent In Room
BRB = Be Right Back	POS = Parent Over Shoulder
CIAO = Goodbye (in Italian)	OTP = On The Phone
CWYL = Chat With You Later	QT = Cutie
CYA = See You	RU = Are You?
CYT or SYT = See You Tomorrow	RU OK = Are you Okay?
EM = Excuse me?	SorG = Straight or Gay
GTG = Got to Go	SWDYT = So What Do You Think?
GUDLUK = Good Luck	TDTM = Talk Dirty To Me
HAK = Hugs And Kisses	THX or TX or THKS = Thanks
ILF = I Love You	TMI = Too Much Information
IMHO = In My Humble Opinion	TOM = Tomorrow
J/K = Just Kidding!	TTYL = Talk to You Later
KOTL = Kiss On The Lips	WTF = What The F***
L8R = Later	WTG = Way to Go
LMK = Let Me Know	WYCM = Will You Call Me?
LOL = Laugh Out Loud	

Multiliteracies: Beyond Text and the Written Word, pages 25–29

It has been argued in recent years that people are becoming less literate. In point of fact, as this book maintains, literacy is simply evolving into new forms—ones that are related but often distinctively different from traditional textuality. Writing as a means of personal communication is being transformed as a result of new technologies such as cellular phones and the Internet. Nowhere is this clearer than in the use of instant messaging by adolescents. Instant messaging, or IM, which usually occurs on the computer, is defined as a form of real-time communication between two or more people based on typed text (Instant messaging and messengers, 2008). Text-messaging, which occurs through more portable, hand-held technologies, is real-time communication with text via one's cell phone or other hand held electronic device.

To fully grasp the evolution of written text in a form such as instant messaging, one must revisit its history. In *Writing Is a Technology that Restructures Thought*, Walter Ong (2001) argues that writing is in fact a technology that has been responsible for establishing critique and focused linear analysis. Ong further states that writing began the separation of the word from the present reality, which was only continued by printing and electronics, thus promoting objectivity and raising our levels of consciousness. However, Ong notes that when writing first came into being, it received much criticism just as advancements in computer technology have today. Plato denoted writing as inhuman, artificial, unresponsive, passive, and outside of the context of struggle where real speech and thought exist.

Text messaging on a cell phone. Photograph by Amanda Goodwin.

This vision of writing as an external, alien technology occurred because no one during Plato's lifetime could have predicted how deeply internalized writing would become. In this context, Ong (2001) argues that properly internalized technology enhances human life rather than degrading it, as is evident in our modern orchestra, where instruments or mechanical inventions allow musicians to "express something poignantly human that cannot" otherwise be expressed.

Ong (2001) concludes his discussion in *Writing Is a Technology that Restructures Thought* with a reflective and thoughtful list of the many benefits writing has given our society—the most fundamental value being the enhancement of separation of the known from the knower, which allows individuals to communicate abstract thought concepts independent of the reality of their use and connection to human life.

The beauty of instant and text messaging is that it has brought the two seemingly divergent worlds of orality and written discourse together as one. No longer is written discourse unresponsive as Plato once argued, nor passive or stagnant for that matter. Written discourse has now crossed the boundaries of being frozen or dead in time. The characteristics once solely held by the world of orality (i.e., mobile, warm, personally interactive) have become an additional component of written discourse.

As with musicians who must internalize the technology of their instruments, making it second nature, so are students internalizing the technology of instant messaging in order to interact with one another in ways that are currently being explored.

Students spend countless hours text messaging and instant messaging. Whether collaborating with other classmates on homework assignments or planning a night at the movies, these methods of communication are increasingly replacing phone calls. Instant messaging, by providing a list of "buddies" that are currently online, allows individuals to communicate without the delay of leaving a message when a friend is not home or having to reach one's friend through intermediaries such as parents or siblings who answer the phone. Instant messaging and text messaging also allow for a message to be sent to multiple people at once, whereas a similar message previously involved multiple phone calls to different households. While these may seem like small nuances, such features of instant messaging and text messaging have revolutionized the way students, and even adults, communicate, read, and write.

One area where instant and text messaging has especially proved beneficial is with the deaf and hard of hearing. These individuals are often delayed in developing their independent living skills due to their parents' con-

A middle-school student using instant messaging to talk to friends. Photograph by Miriam Lipsky.

cern with the child being unable to communicate his or her whereabouts. Tane Akamatsu, Connie Mayer, and Shona Farrelly (2006) have found that two-way text messaging technology has helped alleviate some of the parental concerns that have restricted the development of independence in deaf adolescents. Similarly, in a recent survey of 884 adults with hearing impairments, a majority of the participants used e-mail and instant messaging more often than telecommunications relay services (Bowe, 2002). In this context a form of textuality, instant messaging, comes to replace orality, which at least in terms of traditional spoken language, is something from which deaf individuals have been precluded.

The uses of text messaging is also being explored in treatment programs for college students struggling with issues such as smoking (Obermayer, Riley, & Jean-Mary, 2004), bulimia (Baur, Percevic, Okon, Meermann, & Kordy, 2003), and asthma (Neville, Greene, McLeod, Tracy, & Surie, 2002). Yet a critical area where the impact of instant and text messaging is becoming clearly evident is in the arena where literacy development is most central: education.

Cynthia Lewis and Battina Fabos (2000) investigate research on computer-mediated communication among adolescent females in the Urban Midwest. Although their focus is on the life of one young lady and her best friend, this case study calls for the need for new pedagogies that incorporate "critical frames for new literacies." Furthermore, today's college students are being recognized as part of the "Net Generation." In "Getting Ready for the Net Generation Learner," Kenneth W. Dobbins (2005), president of Southeast Missouri State University, describes a conference he attended entitled *The Key to Competitiveness: Understanding the Next Generation Learner.* This conference was sponsored by the American Association of State Colleges and Universities, and Mr. Dobbins' response to it called for changes in curriculum delivery to meet the technology demands of the "Net Generation."

These advanced communicative technologies are spawning a new approach to education where basic facts and skills are and can no longer be the focus. Anita McAnear (2005) advocates helping students develop the skills necessary to find and use the right tool or information source for the task at hand. Critical thinking is the key.

These explorations are not only occurring in our nation but abroad as well. In Hong Kong, language-specific features in text-based computer-mediated communication (CMC) are being identified and investigated as possible "new literacy practices within the theoretical framework of New Literacy Studies (NLS)" (Lee, 2002).

In addition, the research literature is currently reporting computer-mediated communication (CMC) within university graduate-level programs. As Garrison, Anderson, and Archer (1999) note in "Critical Inquiry in a Text-Based Environment: Computer Conferencing in Higher Education," text-based communication provides time for reflection and thus may actually be preferable to oral communication "when the objective is higher-order cognitive learning" (p. 5). The researchers further develop a conceptual framework for establishing a community of inquiry or critical community of learners via distance education. These researchers note that by fostering communication and collaboration among learners, computer conferencing has initiated a new education movement of distance education (Garrison et al., 1999).

Interactive on-line learning is becoming increasingly prominent in our culture and in our classrooms. It is spawning a new literacy that combines the literacies of our past and present—orality and written discourse—in such an intricate manner that written discourse is flowing more quickly than ever while simultaneously encouraging focused discipline in how we think, communicate, and interact (Garrison et al., 1999).

7

Numbers

Wensen Lin

112358

The first numbers in the Fibonacci series, developed in 1202 by the Italian mathematician Leonardo Fibonacci.

One of the most prevalent and common conceptions of numbers can be found in the following quote by Dedikind that "numbers are free creations of man's mind. They serve as a means of apprehending the difference of things more easily and more sharply" (as cited in Crossley, 1987, p. 2). First developed in primitive societies and ultimately applied in the field of mathematics, numbers manifest an array of empirical functions and contributions from counting to the exploration and advancement of scientific knowledge in human societies.

The use of numbers has been highly valued and extensively exploited in the modern world. For instance, using numbers to sequence or order information found in daily life, such as street addresses, or for identification of placement in competitions (1st, 2nd, etc.) are ways in which numbers are used for non-mathematical purposes to help clarify information that might otherwise be confusing. Additionally, the formation of digitalized identities

Multiliteracies: Beyond Text and the Written Word, pages 31–33

is prevalent in the use of Social Security Numbers, driver's license numbers, credit card numbers, telephone numbers, address numbers, and so on. The omnipresence of numbers in the modern world reflects the common belief that numbers have a culturally universal and timeless status (Crossley, 1987).

While it may be reasonable to assume that the presence of numbers exists to a greater or lesser extent in all cultures, it might be inappropriate to assert that the use of numbers is immune to the influence of culture. The emergence of the modern written Arabic numerals as suggested by Goody (2001) increased people's literacy in the utilization of numbers and affected ways in which knowledge is presented and accumulated.

Parallel to any other forms of literacy, the written and oral presentation of number systems and symbols varies in different social and cultural contexts and at different given points of time in history (Menninger, 1992). Correspondingly, Pither (2002) suggests that the straightforwardness, clarity, and concreteness of numbers tend to become clouded as soon as numbers are applied to nonmathematical subjects. In addition, Crossley (1987) also argued, far from being static or timeless, numbers have continually developed slowly from their earliest concrete beginnings into the sophisticated abstraction of today.

Based on linguistic evidence, not every language has an equal counting vocabulary, with corresponding values and comparable numerals (Menninger, 1992). Additionally, numbers are not neutral and objective, especially where mystical and religious virtues are bestowed upon them in different cultures (Gazalé, 2000). As Schimmel (1994) indicated, numbers have held mystery and meaning since the earliest times and across every society.

Disputing the impartial role of numbers in measuring and quantifying in the mathematical sense is not the purpose of this chapter. Instead it focuses on how numbers, parallel to the traditional conception of literacy as reading and writing, take on an additional role as cultural transmitters of symbolic meanings. In this context, it is important to remember that there are many variations of the symbolization of numbers that are exceptionally sensitive to the uniqueness of the language, religion, and philosophy of a particular culture (Pither, 2002).

Menninger (1992) pointed out that early man, in speech and in writing, drew on his environment for symbols to indicate sizes and quantities; he did not fashion artificial words or symbols to apply only to specific numbers and measures. Pither (2002) believed that the association of numbers and their symbolic meanings could be identified in six broad categories: language, science, art, myth, religion, and culture. It is customary that the interplay between any verbal and visual communication and the above six categories determines the uniqueness of form of literacy across different cultures. There are many examples that illustrate how symbolic meanings of numbers are peculiarly assigned under the influence of the force of some of the above six categories.

In Christian cultures, it would be considered inappropriate to choose "666" as the numbers of one's car license plate. This is because the number "666" is associated with the number of the beast described in the book of Revelation and is considered symbolic of the devil (Hopper, 2000). In contrast, "666" with its similarity in sounds with words meanin "everything goes smoothly" in Chinese is regarded as one of luckiest of all numbers.

The above two examples exhibit the interaction between religion and number meaning, and how number meaning can be closely associated with the linguistic features in different cultures. Conversely, in different cultures, different numbers can be adopted to denote the same notion. For example, in Greece, both 60 and its multiplication, such as 360, were frequently used as "round numbers," whose specific meanings are inflated into the indefinite "many," as in the expression many, many birds (Menninger, 1992). Likewise, 9 and its multiplications play a comparable role in Chinese culture. However, in the *Yi Jing* or the *Book of Changes*, which is a manual of divination, the number 9 is the maximum number, which has no more numbers following it. Influenced by this particular understanding as part of the Chinese tradition, it is usually considered unfavorable to celebrate birthdays at ages ending in 9, such as 19, 29, or 49 because it may imply the end of one's life without any upcoming birthdays.

The above are only a few examples of how numbers take on their symbolic meanings. However, as Pither (2002) has argued, the interpretation of the meaning of numbers is an important, potent and creative force, and a culturally distinct form of literacy.

8

Sign Languages

Communication in a Silent World

Miriam Lipsky

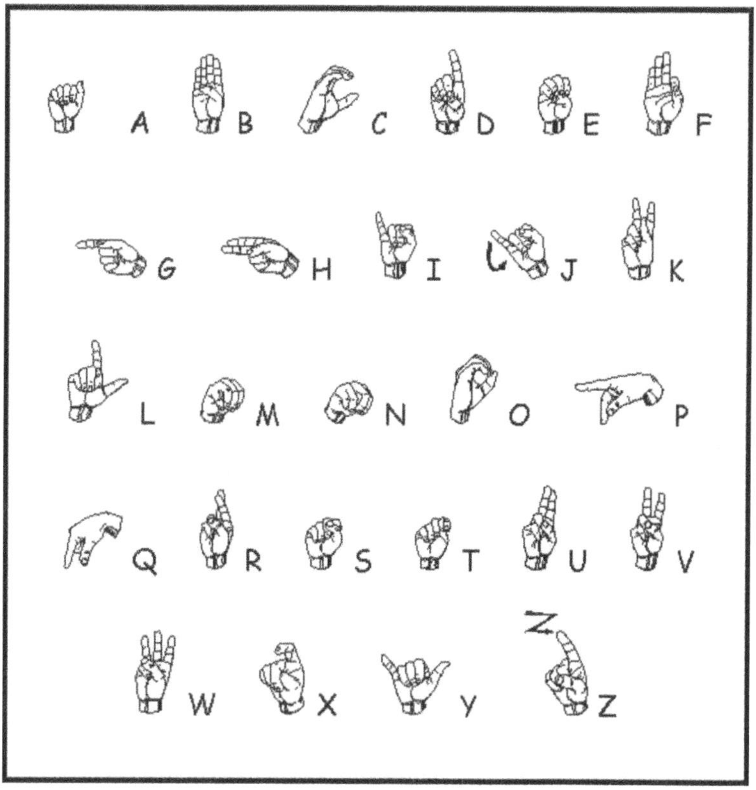

Multiliteracies: Beyond Text and the Written Word, pages 35–39

American Sign Language (ASL) is one of many sign languages used by people who are deaf. In fact, there are over 270 different sign languages, dialects, and sign systems used throughout the world (Harrington, 2006). Although some sign languages follow national boundaries, others do not.

In some countries, deaf people use different sign languages based on the region in which they live or the school they attend, and in other countries the deaf community may have a common sign language with a neighboring country. Sign languages are a powerful alternative literacy for people who are unable to hear. In fact, if we consider literacy, as defined in the Introduction to this book, as the knowledge of letters and the ability to read and write, it will become clear that without sign language(s), deaf people would probably have no pathway to becoming "literate" in the traditional sense at all. It is through sign language, which is the first language of most deaf people, that they are able to begin learning the written language of their native country.

The history of sign languages and the way they have developed is quite interesting. In hearing families where a child is deaf, the child and parents often develop their own form of sign language, sometimes referred to as

"How are you?" hand signed with matching facial expression. Photograph by Eugene F. Provenzo, Jr.

"Friend?" hand signed with matching facial expression. Photograph by Eugene F. Provenzo, Jr.

"home sign," if the parents are not familiar with, or fluent in, ASL or the sign language used in their country or area. None of these unique home languages are formally recognized, but they develop out of necessity to help the parent(s) and child communicate.

No one knows exactly when or where the first "formal" sign language originated. As for American Sign Language, in 1817, a French teacher named Lauren Clerc was brought to the United States by Thomas Gallaudet to help him found the first school for the deaf (the American School for the Deaf) in Hartford, Connecticut. Clerc taught French Sign Language (FSL) to the students at the school, but many of these students already used their own versions of a signed language that had developed naturally (ostensibly various forms of "home sign" referred to earlier). Many people feel that ASL developed out of FSL and the signs that the early students at the American School for the Deaf were using. In any case, ASL has evolved to the point where it shares some elements, notably a great deal of vocabulary, with FSL, but the two languages are mutually unintelligible.

Forty years after the founding of the American School for the Deaf, Thomas Gallaudet's son, Edward Gallaudet, founded the first college for the deaf in 1857, which became Gallaudet University in 1864. Many people unfamiliar with sign language think that it is a translation of the local language. This is far from the truth. While fluent signers are able to use a finger spelling technique to spell out certain proper nouns for which no formal sign exists, actual sign language is a mixture of manual signs (hand shapes, hand movements, and location of the sign in relation to the body), body language/posture, and facial expressions (Battison, 2001). The alphabet used for finger spellings, the manual alphabet, is shown at the beginning of the chapter.

So, if sign language is not a translation of the local language, how does it function from a linguistics standpoint? ASL, like other sign languages, is non-sequential. In spoken language, a sentence follows a linear or sequential format. Because sign languages are spatial, they are non-linear and non-sequential and can convey information using several visual channels simultaneously. For example, suppose I uttered the sentence, "I walked to the park today to meet my friend, and I was happy to see her." This sentence has a sequence of events, first walking, then meeting my friend, and then describing the fact that I was happy to see her. If this same message were signed, the signer could convey walking to the park and being happy to see her friend all as one visual message by combining the signs for walking and then meeting the friend with a happy facial expression.

Research on ASL has shown that linguistically, ASL follows a structure that is similar to the Japanese language, so the grammar and structure of ASL are significantly different from English. This is because the Japanese language, Japanese sign language, and ASL all use what is called a topic-comment grammatical system (Nakamura, 2002). In a topic-comment system, one first states the topic, and then what one is going to say about it. For example, (girl)topic—(throw ball)comment. Interestingly, ASL and British sign language are completely different and mutually unintelligible, even though Americans speak the same language as the British—English. This fact lends further evidence that sign languages are not translations of the local language where they are used.

The use of sign languages has helped people who are deaf and hard of hearing to participate in the literate communities in which they live. In some communities with a high percentage of deaf people, many members of the hearing community have taken the initiative to learn sign language to be able to communicate with their deaf neighbors, friends, family, and customers, as was the case on Martha's Vineyard in the 1800s and early 1900s (Groce, 1985).

Among the deaf community, many do not see their deafness as a disability at all, but rather as a cultural difference. An estimated nine out of ten members of the deaf community in the United States marry other people who are deaf, and many hope to have children who are deaf, so that they may pass on the deaf culture to them, much in the same way that parents of a particular religious or ethnic group would hope to pass on their culture to their children (Deaf Culture, 2008). Quite often, however, deaf people must learn the written language of their country in order to fully participate in the society around them. Unfortunately, deaf students' reading ability lags significantly behind that of their peers (matched for IQ and chronological age), and only 8% of deaf students are able to read above the 4th grade level, likely due to the difficulty of learning English as a second language without the ability to "sound out" new or unfamiliar words (Jackson, Paul, & Smith, 1997).

Sign languages can be used to help translate literate works for deaf people and to help deaf students learn to read printed text. Because sign language is not simply a translation of the local language, learning the local spoken and/or printed language is like learning a second language for a deaf person, with the additional challenge of a lack of auditory input. Much in the same way as an instructor might translate a difficult vocabulary word for a student who is learning English as a second language, a teacher of the deaf might use sign language to translate a difficult vocabulary word for a deaf student. There are even signing "avatars" in special software that can translate words into sign language for children who are learning to read a printed language using a computer. Hopefully by using these new technologies and techniques, deaf students will be able to increase their ability to communicate with the hearing community and to read and comprehend the written works of their "second language."

9

Tattoos

The Power of Ink

Jennifer Diptee

"Koi Tattoo" photographed by Jason Griffin.

Multiliteracies: Beyond Text and the Written Word, pages 41–44

Within our current historical context it is impossible to narrow the term *literacy* to mean just the ability to read and write. As has already been discussed in this book, many of these alternate or multiliteracies require a broader scope of what is meant by communication, expression, meaning, and ultimately literacy. To further exemplify the presence of multiliteracies, this chapter examines the culture of tattoos and its significance as a type of literacy.

Similar to the roadside memorials for people killed in automobile accidents or the emoticon symbols typed on a computer that convey emotions to others, tattoos offer a visual mode of representation that carry with them deep emotions and beliefs. While the messages may not be fully understood by all, they are valued in different society circles and often require a degree of literacy in deciphering.

Tattooing is a visual literacy, rife with symbolic codes and collective memory. It is more than an art because it is readable and readily interpreted by many. Its history is as ancient as the oral tradition, first used by primitive cultures and then imported to Western societies. It is a living language whose permanence cannot be denied or extinguished and whose universality and continuity with the past as well as effectiveness in communicating ideas is undeniable. Not unlike oral tradition, it has evolved according to the social, economic, and cultural circumstances of society. Within that evolution it has been redefined, mapped and re-mapped, and gone through various stages of acceptance and repudiation. It has been stigmatized as practiced by marginalized groups such as "carnies," criminals, and convicts, and then it has also been fully accepted by the middle and upper classes, as well as been used by underground groups and counter-cultures (Lentini, 1999). The permanency of tattooing is based on the fact that the typically wordless symbols used are imbued with significant meaning and are sported by diverse peoples who, regardless of language, have communicated their message to fellow countrymen and across boundaries (De Mello, 2000).

Tattoos have been around for centuries, with each culture modifying them accordingly to their social context. For instance, there is archeological evidence that the origin of tattooing in Japan can be traced back to the Jomon period (10,000 B.C.–300 B.C.). This is amazing when one takes into consideration that it was not until the 8th century that the first Japanese printed books appeared. In Japanese history alone, we learn that tattoos were used to convey different meanings and served different functions: they helped make distinctions between social classes (as minority groups called eta carried certain marks), served as punishment and branding of social outcasts and criminals during the 16th century (where criminals were marked with a black ring around an arm or forehead for each offense), were seen as

Tattoo by Panupong Wongphan, Thailand tattoo artist, 2006. Photographed by Plai.

signs of virtue and purity among the Ainu and Ryukyu tribes, reflected a rite of passage into sexual maturity and marriage for women, or were seen as marks of courage and pride amongst samurai warriors (Yamada, 2000). In fact, while tattoos are now legal, they are still considered negative in Japan today due to the historical background they retain. According to Bell and Valentine (cited in Lentini, 1999), a body decorated with tattoos is a political statement because it causes reactions and counter-actions from the state as forces within and outside the individual struggle for power and control. Hence, tattoos carry bold statements (i.e., resistance, dominion, contradiction, upheaval, satisfaction, etc.) that can be read and understood, perhaps more vividly than traditional literacy.

One example of political voice in tattooing is choosing to sport a tattoo of Che Guevara, which is encumbered with intellectual baggage and literal messages from those who wear it to those who see it. The viewer either recoils or accepts the image, but the reaction always has political and social implications. People who know of his political doings will flinch from that person based on the injustices attributed to Guevara, while those who see him as a "sacred" figure and venerate him will accept the message.

Perhaps nowhere else has the political side of tattooing been more interesting than in its use by Russian prisoners during the Soviet era. In what can be considered an extremely complex and secret way of tattooing, inmates inked satirical and offensive symbols that portrayed messages where certain marks revealed an inmate's rank within the criminal social order. This unspoken communication through visual representation informed the world (i.e., the criminal environment) of one's past or one's associations. According to Danzig Baldaev (2004), a Russian prison guard who documented over forty years of images and their meanings, tattoos embodied "a thief's complete service record, his entire biography" (Baldaev, 2004, p. 27). Symbols explained what type of illegal work was done, accomplishments and failures, as well as jails a thief had served in. One such example was the tattoo reading "Heil Hitler!" which did not have an association to the political head or movement but which represented a "thief's attitude of denial or the symbol of refusal" to submission (Baldaev, 2006, p.33). Research on criminal tattoos reveal that there is a vast list of symbols that contain specific meanings and understandings, that when used, ultimately empower prisoners. The tattoo message reveals a certain control over their environment that can be understood by those around them (Forbis, 1994). This suggests some of the reasons why youths—particularly disenfranchised youths—have frequently made tattoos such an important part of their cultural expression as a symbol of resistance and rebellion.

Lastly, an important feature to note about the tattoo community is that, similar to other types of literacy, it has created its own set of jargon. Words such as *body suit, sleeved, jailhouse,* or *memorial tattoo* are part of a lexicon utilized by those who provide or seek tattoos in a manner that is understood across environments. Knowledge of the appropriate terminology allows for the sharing of ideas and information about a collective interest (Krakow, 1994).

In conclusion, not only does the culture of tattoos represent a type of graphic expression, but also through presenting and deciphering messages, tattooing provides a function of empowerment. Tattoos are a visual communication and type of literacy that should be acknowledged for more than the traditional stereotypes they harbor, but rather for the social and political power they provide. They carry a sense of information regarding group membership, defiance to authority, or an ideological stance that requires a certain amount of literacy to be deciphered and understood. An awareness of how this type of literacy impacts students in our classrooms allows educators to acknowledge the social intelligence that students bring with them.

10

The Lectore

Reading Aloud as a Collective Literacy

Eugene F. Provenzo, Jr.

A Medieval Classroom.

In *A is for Ox: The Collapse of Literacy and the Rise of Violence in an Electronic Age,* Barry Sanders (1995) describes one of his young college students, "Maxwell," who suffered from such severe reading problems (because

Multiliteracies: Beyond Text and the Written Word, pages 45–47

of dyslexia) that his high school advisors cautioned him against going to college. After interviewing him, however, the Claremont Colleges accepted him on a probational basis into their undergraduate program.

Maxwell did remarkably well in his four years at school and graduated with his B.A., despite the fact that he had not, strictly speaking, read one book or written a single paper. Instead, his friends read to him whatever he was studying. He would then summarize what he had learned to see if he had understood what had been read to him.

Sanders (1995) describes Maxwell as a "literate young man":

> His sentences sparkle. He can hear a clunker because he is so finely tuned to rhythm. He delights in that sense of pleasure as an argument nears its inevitable conclusion. In class, he fired off witty wisecracks that brought class into focus. His friends called him The Punster. He claims Puck and Huck as distant cousins. He is as articulate and wonderfully devilish as Huck. His dyslexia had permitted him to drop out of the competition without irritating his parents. On the contrary, he got lots of attention. He became a well-mannered gang of one. (p. 231)

According to Sanders, Maxwell and his friends had created a close-knit community. Members of the community who knew how to read and write would

"Man hired by cigar workers to read to them as they work, Tampa, Fla." Lewis Hine, photographer. Photographic print. 1909 Jan. Courtesy of the Library of Congress.

gather around him and other interested individuals and read to them from a book or some other printed material.

Sanders refers to this process as "alphabetization." Through the shared reading of a text the group involved not only became more intimately connected, but they shared in a collective analysis and interpretation of ideas. According to Sanders, someone like Maxwell should not be treated like "an inferior illiterate." Instead, "The words have been freed from the page and turned back into orality so that everyone in the group can more equally hear and understand" (Sanders, 1995, p. 231).

Maxwell was involved in what historians of literacy have described as "textual communities." During the Middle Ages, this type of textual community was typified by a scholar, surrounded by a group of students, to whom he recited a text, which they would then analyze and discuss.

During the nineteenth and early twentieth centuries, it was a common practice for some industrial workers, such as cigar rollers, to hire a "reader" or "lectore" to read a text to them while they worked. In most instances the workers who listened were textually illiterate. Yet, despite this, they became critically involved in the content of what was being read. In the case of textually illiterate Cuban cigar rollers, they were often among the most politically educated and engaged figures in the revolution against Spain that eventually led to the Spanish American War.

In an age of educational accountability there seems to be little time for shared experiences in reading and orality. Teachers rarely read aloud to students anymore. Memorizing poetry out loud, a common practice in the nineteenth and even early twentieth centuries, is a largely forgotten custom. What opportunities for literacy and learning have been lost as a result?

Sanders argues that by defining literacy as only textual or "reading instruction" we construct what amounts to a highly narrow and limiting model of literacy. According to Sanders, literacy is not something to be unlocked just by opening up books, but can be expanded to include much more than just reading and writing. As we emerge into an increasingly postmodern culture, it is clear that precisely this phenomenon is at work.

11

Rap Music

A Socio-Cultural Revolution

Maribel G. Harder

Hip Hop artist raps on the street in Philadelphia, PA. Photograph by Amanda Goodwin.

Multiliteracies: Beyond Text and the Written Word, pages 49–54

According to J. L. Lemke (1998), literacies consist of a group of mutually dependent social practices that connect people, media, objects, and strategies to make meaning. Moreover Lemke (1998) states that all literacy is multimedia, such that meaning is not made with language alone, but instead with visual or vocal understanding of the linguistic signs that provide non-linguistic meanings such as tone of voice. Lemke continues to describe literacies as always being social and advocates the learning of a combination of other modes of literacy, such as singing, drawing, or mime with writing in order to enhance communication. In fact, he proposes that meaning is most effectively enhanced through the union of "typological" (i.e., the way language operates) and "topological" (i.e., visual perception and spatial gesturing such as drawing and dancing) modes of meaning-making.

Rap music, a form of art and communication that has become exponentially successful and popular among American youth of all backgrounds in recent years, is a prime example of such a literacy practice that, contrary to popular adult opinion, can prove to be very beneficial and positive for the social and individual growth and development of today's teens and young adults. It represents an alternative or multiliteracy in American culture.

Rapping in hip hop music is believed to have evolved from the "griots," folk poets that originated in West Africa centuries ago (Rapping, 2008). Also

Kool G Rap and The Game in 2006. Courtesy of Wikipedia Commons.

Griots de Sambala, roi de Médine (illustration de *Côte occidentale d'Afrique* du Colonel Frey), 1890.

known as "troubadour(s)" or "storyteller(s)", the griots combined entertainment with education by reciting tribal history and current events to audiences (Powell, 1991). Their performances were often enhanced with "satirical asides, proverbs, jokes, praise, and ridicule" (Powell, 1991, p. 246).

As part of the tradition of oral recitation that began in Africa many centuries ago, modern-day rap music surfaced in the 1970s from the streets of inner-city neighborhoods, reflecting the hopes, concerns, and aspirations of urban black youth (Powell, 1991). Rap is speech that contains complex cadences, intricate poetic forms, and inventive wordplay (Rapping, 2008). Key components of rap include flow, rhythmic delivery, and rhyme. In fact, rap has been referred to as a form of rhymed storytelling (Rose, 1994). "Flow" refers to the rhythm and beat of a particular artist or MC. This flow values large sets of rhyming syllables which include consonance, assonance, half rhyme, and internal rhyme such that rappers are known for their distinctive style of rhyming (Rapping, 2008). Rap music also encompasses the various forms of wordplay evident in classical poetry such as double entendres and alliteration. Similarly, rap music also reflects themes associated with traditional poetry, yet expands on these themes to convey the street life from which hip hop culture surfaced (Rapping, 2008).

In the early 1970s, the group The Last Poets emerged, forming "a dominant prototype for later rap artists" (Powell, 1991, p. 246). The Last Poets "took street corner rap and used it as an assault on racism, Black self-exploitation, and stereotyped racial roles" (Powell, 1991, p. 246). During the disco era, rap became popular with the street gangs in urban centers such as Harlem and the South Bronx in New York City (Powell, 1991). Rappers worked with DJs, switching back and forth to mix the best parts of the music (Powell, 1991).

For many, the advent of the group Public Enemy (PE) in 1987 marked the emergence of rap as a political cultural form (Rose, 1991). This group spoke of pride in oneself and black unity. "Public Enemy's success opened the door to more politically and racially explicit material" (Rose, 1991, p. 276). Religious rap has also come to being, with Christian rap currently being the most commercially successful of the forms. Rap is now crossing racial barriers with the advent of white rappers such as Eminem, who is of Scottish descent and the Beastie Boys, a highly successful rap group composed of white Jewish teenagers.

Unfortunately, due to much publicity and commercial success, when many think of rap only one form of rap comes to mind: "Gangsta" rap with its explicit, lewd lyrics that glorify violence and hedonism. According to Tricia Rose (1991) of Rutgers University, the focus of associating rap music with violence is in fact a result of calculated decisions made by police reports and the media in an effort to obliterate a movement that has the potential to empower historically oppressed African American youth, which would be a threat to the stability of mainstream society. Rose states that "ideological power and resistance is exercised through signs and language" (Rose, 1991, p. 277). She further notes that hip hop artists articulate a range of

Beastie Boys at the Big Day Out concert in Melbourne, Australia. Photograph by JstJohn, courtesy of Wikipedia Commons.

counter-reactions to the assortment of institutional policing faced by many young African Americans, and that "venue resistance to rap music is driven both by economic calculations and the hegemonic media interpretation of rap's fans, music, and concert-related violence" (Rose, 1991, p. 284). These false and exaggerated media interpretations mask "the source of discursive and institutional power by directing attention away from blatant and active forces of discrimination and fueling racially motivated control efforts by the police" (Rose, 1991, p. 284) and other institutions.

Rose cites the cultural theorist bell hooks' view on rap, stating that its "capacity as a form of testimony and an articulation of the young, Black, urban critical voice has profound potential as a language of liberation and social protest" (Rose, 1991, p. 289). Dierdre Glenn Paul (2000) further states that due to its ability to raise levels of consciousness, "rap is a viable site for the practice of critical media literacy", where individuals can understand how the print and nonprint texts evident in their everyday lives can 'help to construct their knowledge of the world and the various social, economic, and political positions they occupy within it" (p. 249; citing Alvermann, Moon, & Hagood, 1999).

Edgar H. Tyson (2002) further contends that positive and negative rap exist, and all too often "rap music has been presented and perceived very negatively by the media and the larger society" (p. 142). His argument in "Hip Hop Therapy: An Exploratory Study of a Rap Music Intervention with At-risk and Delinquent Youth" is that positive rap music depicts solutions and inspires to improve unwanted conditions, uplifts people, and raises their consciousness. As a result, integrating this music into therapy with at-risk students may, according to Tyson, provide a powerful means by which to engage at-risk youth and enhance their self-esteem, identity, and development.

Based on well-established therapeutic techniques such as bibliotherapy (a technique in poetry therapy that utilizes literature to facilitate treatment) and music therapy, Edgar Tyson (2002) explored the therapeutic qualities of rap music intervention with a selected group of youth using a randomized experimental design. In keeping with J. T. Pardeck's (1994) stages of bibliotherapy, he "selected a series of rap recordings that would create discussion specifically on issues of self-concept, positive racial identity, group identity, and peace and unity" (Tyson, 2002, p. 135).

The study lacked statistical power for quantitative analysis due to the small sample size of 11 youth (five in the experimental group and six in the comparison group). However, the qualitative analysis in this study yielded very interesting results. All five group members of the Hip Hop Therapy (HHT) group stated that they enjoyed the group sessions more than any previous group session they had been involved in at their shelter. All the group members also expressed excitement and enthusiasm for the group sessions and pleaded with the author to continue using the approach after the experiment was over. In addition, four of the youth expressed a desire to create, share and discuss their own rap songs with the group. Interestingly, four other youth in the shelter expressed displeasure for not being allowed to participate in the HHT sessions (Tyson, 2002).

Thus, Tyson argues that HHT is a model that warrants further research with larger sample sizes. Citing W. D. Holman (1996), Tyson clarifies the need to incorporate the approach with specificity of music, intervention, and cliental in order to yield the most positive results.

More recently, Susan Weinstein (2007) has profiled four young writers and rappers, ages 15 to 21, in order to explore how enjoyment in composing, culture, and out-of-school literacy can affect in-school engagement and achievement. She concludes her research, stating, "Focusing on the intricacies of a genre that gives so many young people so much pleasure, and in which they participate so enthusiastically, can only enrich our understandings of how and why engagements with literacy develop" (Weinstein, 2007, p. 281).

Furthermore, in this new millennium, where rap music, under the umbrella of hip hop, has actually reached popularity beyond racial groups, Bakari Kitwana (2005) affirms that by including hip hop in mainstream American culture, both black and white American youth can explore new ideas together.

In conclusion, rap, as an alternative form of literacy, is giving rise to new racial politics that have never been seen before. The possibilities for positive social transformation are significant as the hip hop culture unites races with the first generation of Americans that live free from defacto segregation (Kitwana, 2005). In this global era in which we live, where many are calling for a socio-cultural approach to literacy (i.e., Lankshear, Cushman, Kroll), rap music cannot be overlooked as an arena in which learners can "critically explore significant issues attached to language, culture, and power" (Paul, 2000, p. 251) through culturally relevant texts.

12

Corporate Logos

William B. Deese

Apple Corporation's logo on their new store in Boston. Photograph by Phil Laeger.

Multiliteracies: Beyond Text and the Written Word, pages 55–57

The term *logo*, which has its origin in the ancient Greek term *logotipos*, is defined as "a graphic element, symbol, or icon of a trademark or brand" (Logos, 2007). As key visual devices that cause immediate recognition of a company, these iconic symbols represent specific identities that are linked to products and services for companies and are therefore important components of marketplace identities. With businesses competing in increasingly global economies, logo uniqueness is essential to avoiding confusion. Individuals must be able to read these logos in order to ascertain indices of quality that are associated with certain companies. As a result, knowledge of logos is a necessary postmodern alternative literacy for consumers.

For students, exposure to logos is one of their first experiences with environmental print. At an early age, children can identify meanings that correspond to logos and symbols. "Logos and text on cereal boxes, milk cartons, billboards, household items [etc]...all contribute to an understanding that groups of letters stand for objects" (Manning, 2004, p. 78). This knowledge of print provides building blocks on which to build more complex understanding of literacy. Teachers have even found that using group and class word-logo matching activities help students connect knowledge of logos as literacy to general word literacy (Xu & Rutledge, 2003).

Although there are tens of thousands of corporations who use an emblem as a logo, only a small percentage are recognized without a name. As a multiliteracy, corporate logos require the viewer to be familiar with the icon, and corporations in recent times have learned that their success and growth is dependent upon this consumer recognition. Often lesser-known emblems of companies are accompanied by the name of the corporation in an attempt to build the consumer recognition that more well-known corporations enjoy.

Corporate logos are like symbols used in other forms of communication that, when well-established, are able to transcend the difficulties normally associated with written language. When these corporations expand into new linguistic or cultural regions, their symbol or logo represents the products and/or services that the company offers. For those who are familiar with the symbol, meaning is established, and the barriers of linguistic differences are overcome. Populations of consumers may not be familiar with the language of the country in which the company is established and headquartered, but the universality of the meaning behind the logo nevertheless allows those who understand the meaning(s) represented with the logo to engage in immediate recognition. Companies in postmodern society have placed increasing importance on the design of their logos because they have come to acknowledge that their logo, "is not just an image,

Nike's corporate "swoosh" brands their shoes. Photograph by Darius Monsef.

it is the embodiment of the organization" (Logos, 2007), and thus they must protect their image through registration as a trademark. Examples of companies that have established this superior level of logo recognition include Apple Inc.'s apple with a bite out of it, Chevrolet's horizontal cross, and Nike's "swoosh." For individuals who encounter these images, they immediately engage in a form of meaning translation, enabling both the company and the consumer to use this multiliteracy to predict the quality of the products offered. Students bring understanding of the power of logos with them to the classroom, heightening their awareness and dependence on symbols and logos in creating meaning from their environment.

13

AIDS Quilt as a Literacy

Lisa Repaskey

The AIDS quilt at the National Mall. Photograph courtesy of the NAMES Project Foundation.

Cleve Jones, a San Francisco community activist, picked up the San Francisco Chronicle on Thanksgiving, 1985, and read a horrifying headline on what was supposed to be a day of thanks. The headline announced that 1,000 San Franciscans were dead from AIDS (Hawkins,

Multiliteracies: Beyond Text and the Written Word, pages 59–63

1993; Stull, 2001). It was coincidental that, on that same day, Jones was coordinating the annual Harvey Milk Candlelight Memorial March, which commemorates the life and work of San Francisco's first openly gay supervisor who was gunned down in 1978 along with then-San Francisco mayor George Moscone (NAMES Project AIDS Memorial Quilt, 2007). Cleve Jones had lost countless friends to AIDS, and realized that many people who would be participating in the march also would have lost loved ones to AIDS. Very little was being done to combat the spread of the disease because, at this time in U.S. history, the American government chose to blame gays for contracting AIDS because of their lifestyle choices instead of considering AIDS a public health issue (Stull, 2001). Jones wondered who would remember those fellow Americans that have been lost to AIDS after they were gone (Stull, 2001).

At the march, Jones asked the marchers to carry a placard with the name of someone they knew who had died from AIDS as they marched

A single panels of the AIDS quilt. Photograph courtesy of the NAMES Project Foundation.

"Tzompantli" courtesy of David Robles.

through the streets of San Francisco. When the marchers got to the San Francisco Federal Building, Cleve Jones asked the marchers to tape their placards to the outside wall of the building in an effort to protest the government's lack of response to the AIDS crisis (Hawkins, 1993; Stull, 2001). It was a powerful image. In that moment, with the simple act of viewing so many names of those who had lost their lives to AIDS, it "exposed both private loss and public indifference" (Hawkins, 1993).

That powerful image of the simplicity of just a basic listing of the names of those who perished from AIDS became the catalyst for the creation of the AIDS quilt. Each quilt panel is 3' × 6', roughly the size of a human grave, a living "footprint" of a human life. The individual squares of the AIDS quilt became a living memorial to remember and honor those who died of the disease.

> When, during the Aztec Empire, the priests performed their ritual sacrifice... they would take the skulls of the victims, make holes in the temples and fix them onto long poles which they would string up in front of the big pyramid in such a way that whoever stood on top of the pyramid could look down as they imagined the gods would, and could count the skulls on

> a device called a tzompantli. They literally imagined the gods counting the sacrifices.... And this is what the Quilt is for AIDS. You display the Quilt, horizontally, to the gods so they can see when enough people have been sacrificed and send the message, 'Stop the sacrifice!' This is exactly the same as the tzompantli. You are displaying the equivalent of the skulls to the gods so they can decide when there are enough." (Young, 1997, quote from Dr. Casper Schmidt)

Materials used to create the quilt squares are very personal and extraordinarily profound in the story that they tell about the lives of each individual who was lost to this horrific disease. Families and friends of those people who have died from AIDS utilize a wide range of materials that tell the deeply intimate story of that beloved person, not necessarily with words alone, but with special totemic items that represent the life of this loved one. Materials used to make the quilt squares may include photographs, decorative items, fabrics, and favorite clothing items, as well as profoundly personal items such as wedding bands, awards, or human hair. Occasionally, more unique items are also used in the making of the quilt square such as a bowling ball, condoms, stuffed animals, or even the cremated ashes of the loved one in whose reverent memory the quilt square was created (NAMES Project AIDS Memorial Quilt, 2007).

Each quilt square is uniquely crafted to tell the world the story, in symbolic literacy, of the person whose life was cut tragically short due to AIDS. According to Lugliani (1996), together, these quilt squares comfort loved ones while recording how life is lived during the time of the AIDS epidemic. The AIDS Memorial Quilt, by showing the uniqueness of each human life, calls for compassionate and rational responses to the AIDS crisis and demands that leaders take action to end the dying.

The AIDS quilt was first displayed in its entirety in 1987 in Washington, DC, with approximately 2,000 panels. Approximately half a million people attended the event, including about 55,000 school children (GLINN Media, n.d.). The AIDS quilt would visit Washington, DC a total of five more times. The last visit was in 1996, with over two million visitors.

As of the end of 2006, the AIDS quilt's size measured over 46,000 panels (3' × 6' panels) with more than 91,000 names. If it were to be shown in its entirety again, the AIDS quilt would cover the equivalent of 26 football fields, and if laid end to end, it would stretch more than 50 miles (Stull, 2001). Since the first quilt square was made, over 15 million visitors have come to witness the powerful message of the AIDS quilt (NAMES Project AIDS Memorial Quilt, 2007). "The Quilt has redefined the tradition of quilt-making in response to contemporary circumstances. A memorial, a tool for

A single panels of the AIDS quilt. Photograph courtesy of the NAMES Project Foundation.

education and a work of art, the Quilt is a unique creation, an uncommon and uplifting response to the tragic loss of human life" (aidsquilt.org).

The AIDS Memorial Quilt represents a multiliteracy that communicates the personal stories of AIDS victims as well as the overall picture of the significant loss of life from AIDS. Each unique quilt square is a narrative biography of a life cut tragically short, leaving behind a totemic "footprint" and giving voice to the now-voiceless victims of AIDS in order for the world to stop and take notice of this horrible, life-robbing disease.

14

Nautical and Aeronautical Literacies

Gabriel Quintana

A Crow's Nest. English Wikipedia 2005, September 8, 2005. Courtesy of Malcolm Morley.

Multiliteracies: Beyond Text and the Written Word, pages 65–68

Many scientific and practical fields have a unique vocabulary. These vocabularies provide operational terms that are critical in conducting practical activities in the field. An example of this can be seen in naval and aeronautical navigation. Naval and aeronautical terms are often closely related. Bearing, for example, is used by both sailors and pilots, as are rudder and yaw. Although similar, each area also has its own specialized terms. Naval terms include: kedge, half hitch, and ketch. Aeronautical terms include aileron, spoiler, Vertical Sight Indicator (VSI), and Very High Frequency Omni Directional Range Finder (VOR). This chapter will explore five of the many associations that form the codex of naval and aeronautical literacies.

The first component forming this codex is the terminology used in naval and aeronautical operations. These terms did not arise from a codified or mandated structure; instead they developed as a result of the merging of many different nautical and aeronautical traditions. In the compendium, *The Origin of Navy Terminology*, the Department of the Navy (2006) addresses the historical development of naval language. One such example is how the term crow's nest originated from the use of a crow caged in a ship's lookout tower that was released for sighting land when poor visibility was present. The reason for the crow's use is that the bird would always head for land, and therefore would act as a guide for the ship and its navigators (Department of the Navy, 2006). Aviation terminology has similar historical origins. For example, the term pushing the envelope comes from the pilot's constant testing of an airplane's limits as described in the aircraft's performance envelope, which is the report of its engineering limits (Moreland, 1998).

A second component of naval and aeronautical literacy is the appropriate knowledge of nature. In the yearly published nautical volume, *Chapman Piloting: Seamanship & Small Boat Handling*, Maloney (1999) stresses the importance of understanding nature by looking at weather patterns, such as cloud movements and wind shifts, as well as the understanding of tides and currents. Appreciating the components of weather and tides is essential for a seaman's success (Maloney, 1999). Likewise, airplane pilots need to heed the directives of weather and air currents. A good pilot is able to distinguish "good air" (i.e., air that is not turbulent) from "bad air" (i.e., turbulent and unsteady air) and is able to adjust for the comfort and safety of the passengers aboard his airplane. Illman (1995) suggests that even landings and takeoffs are influenced by the natural terrain on which an airplane is attempting to navigate, such as asphalt's retention and emission of latent heat that tends to raise a plane's nose on landing.

The third part of the codex of naval and aeronautical literacies is knowledge of the craft's limitations. For example, a sailor must know his or her

Cessna F172G at Kemble Airfield, Gloucestershire, England, July 2005. Courtesy of Adrian Pingstone.

boat's limits when dealing with strong winds so that the ship does not tip over or that the sails do not rip (Maloney, 1999). Also, it is important for a skipper to navigate a sailboat in the right direction even when the wind is not blowing in the path of his or her destination. Aircraft pilots must be aware of the fastest speed an airplane is able to fly without damaging the fuselage and know the maximum payload of the aircraft to ensure correct lift (Illman, 1995).

The fourth element of nautical and aeronautical literacies is the symbols commonly employed in sea and air navigation. For instance, ships often use flags to relay messages or display their nationality. Further, the combination of nautical flags can form whole words and phrases, allowing for communication without the use of a wireless transmitter. At night, which is normally extremely dark in the middle of the ocean, lights on a boat indicate its moving, direction, and relative speed (Ludins, 1980). Symbols are also widely present in aeronautics; the registry painted on the side of an airplane indicates its national registration. For instance, the number "G-BGMP" indicates that the airplane is from the United Kingdom (G) (Illman, 1995).

The fifth and final element that makes up the codex of naval and aeronautical literacies is the interpretation of navigational aids. Both ship captains and aircraft pilots rely on the use of charts to aid their navigation, such as showing the location of lighthouse beacons or exhibiting the correct flight pattern in restricted airspace to attempt a safe landing. A related aid

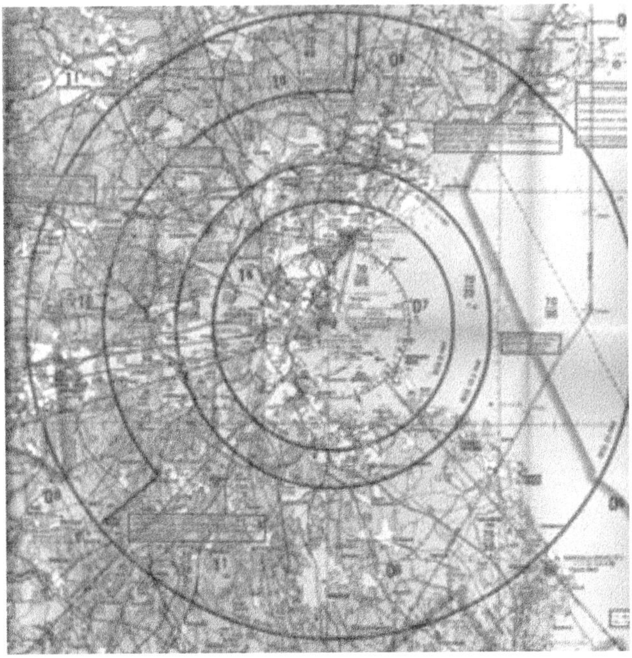

Air Traffic Control Chart. Courtesy of National Aeronautical Charting Office.

to navigation is the Global Positioning System (GPS), which indicates the exact position of an aircraft or watercraft anywhere on the globe. The GPS has replaced many other aids to navigation, such as the LORAN system, the compass, the sextant, and the Very High Frequency Omnidirectional Range (VOR) system (Illman, 1995).

What do these codes tell us about the nature of technical literacies? First and foremost, technical literacies are diverse. The five literacies outlined above constitute very different ways of knowing and communicating. Implied in the idea of their diversity is their complexity. Naval and aeronautical systems combine varied systems into a single system. It is interesting that while these systems are complex, they are often learned and employed informally. In this context, an important characteristic of alternative or multiliteracies can be seen—that is, the informal context in which these literacies are assimilated or learned, and the sophistication of the concepts or literacies that are at work.

15

Scientific Simulation

Kathryn LeRoy

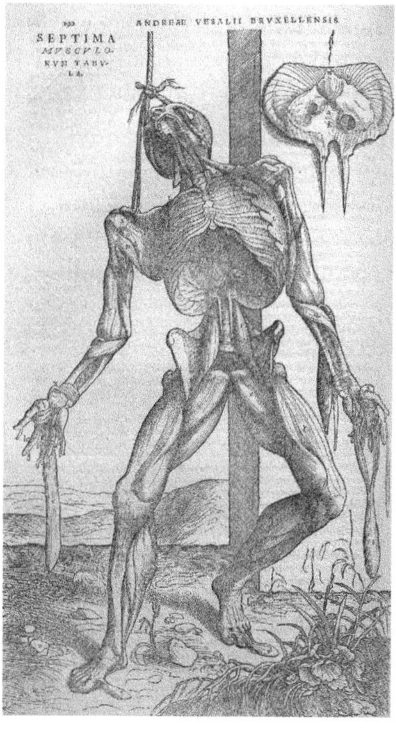

Andrea Vesalius (1514–1564), in his celebrated anatomy book *Fabrica,* included many detailed drawings of human anatomy, essentially creating on paper a simulation of the human body. Courtesy of the Wikipedia Commons.

Multiliteracies: Beyond Text and the Written Word, pages 69–72

New technologies bring with them the need to develop new literacies. This is certainly the case with simulations. Simulations—specifically computer simulations—are computer programs designed to model or replicate a particular system. Computer simulations are rapidly becoming the principal tool of scientific and mathematical modeling in physics, chemistry, earth science, and biology. Computer simulations are also being used to model systems in economics, psychology, and the social sciences.

Simulations go back to antiquity. Provenzo (in press) contends that the development of modern painting and book illustrations during the Renaissance period represents attempts to substitute models or simulations for actual things—such as maps representing the world, engravings representing places, or anatomical etchings representing the human body. Computer simulations, however, are a relatively new phenomenon. Their beginning probably has its origins with the Manhattan Project in World War II, when simulations were used to help model the mechanisms for the Defense Department's detonation of the first atomic bomb (Computer simulation, 2008).

In the sixty years since the first detonation of a nuclear bomb, computer simulations have redefined how the study of science is conducted. As computers have become more accessible and cheaper, they have also increasingly come into use in schools. Simulations are now an important part of many science education programs and represent an important

Picture taken of atomic bombing at Nagasaki on August 9, 1945. Picture courtesy of the Library of Congress Prints and Photographs Division.

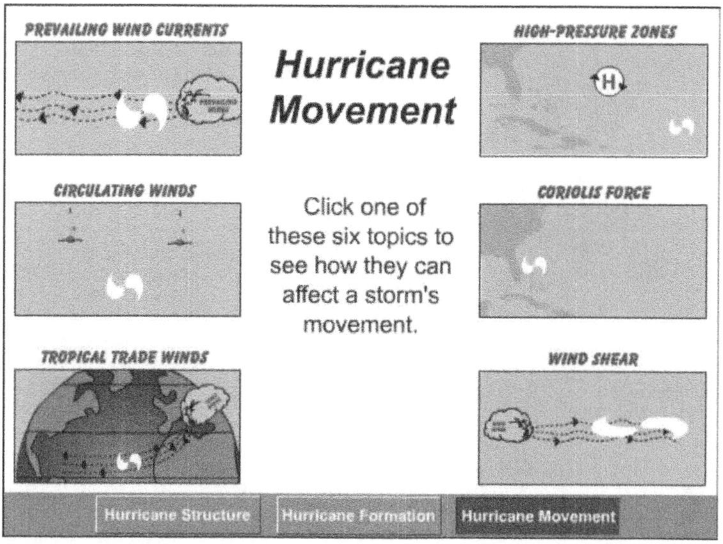

An example of an online hurricane simulation developed by NASA.

new emerging literacy. The National Science Education Standards, for example, recommend that students experience making observations, posing questions, planning investigations, reviewing experimental evidence, and interpreting data to answer important scientific issues (National Research Council, 1996). Computer simulations can provide the foundation for such experiences.

Does the use of computer simulations actually increase student learning? The work of Jean Piaget and his learning theories assumes that there are two ways to structure knowledge. The first is assimilation—fitting new ideas into existing configurations. The second is accommodation or reorganizing the existing knowledge structure so that new ideas fit into it. Piaget's theory that a learner has to work with concepts of concrete objects and events before the ability to think abstractly has an impact on today's teaching practice (Marzano, 1998). In other words, science instruction that begins with concrete objects and hands-on activities and is slow to transition to greater abstractions represents Piaget's theories in practice.

Simulation software provides concrete models of the type seen necessary for learning by Piaget. As more and more software products become available, so does the vast number of science topics that have computer simulations. Examples of topics range from DNA fingerprinting to global warming to atomic structure to energy systems to frog dissections. The potential benefits of using these products include not only increasing student

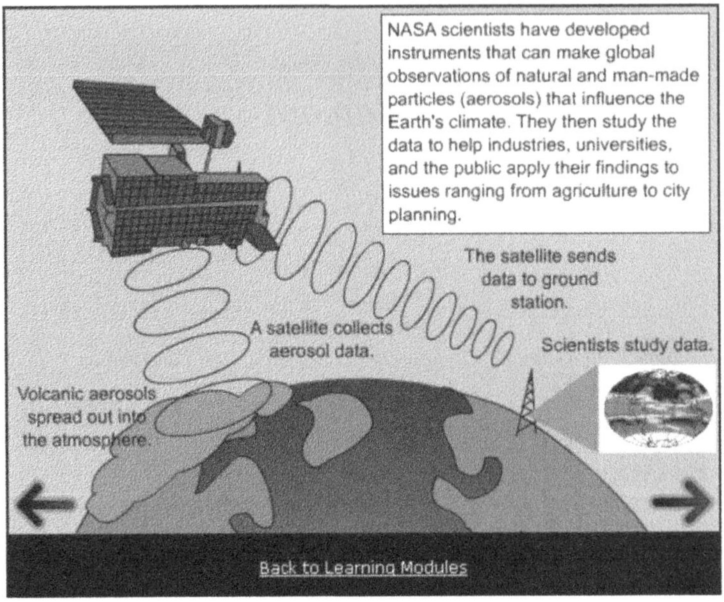

An example of an online atmospheric simulation from NASA.

excitement about learning, but also reducing classroom laboratory and equipment costs, avoiding the need to address ethical considerations involved in doing animal dissections, saving classroom instructional time, and providing visual representations of scientific phenomena that students may otherwise not experience.

With benefits come cautions as well. It is crucial as new and innovative computer simulations reach the science classroom that there is ongoing evaluation of the accuracy of the simulation in promoting science content. As the French theorist Jean Baudrillard (1983) suggests, the simulation may lead us into a situation where we confuse the model for the reality. The fact seems clear, that in the twenty-first century simulations will not only be used more and more in teaching, but they will increasingly define and shape our understanding of the world. In doing so, it will be necessary to understand the implications of this technology, and its role in shaping the scientific literacy of new learners.

16

Streaming Messages

William B. Deese

Fox news channel program with a streaming message running along the bottom of the screen. Photograph by Amanda Goodwin.

Multiliteracies: Beyond Text and the Written Word, pages 73–76

One of the most common forms of digital texts found today, streaming messages, had its beginnings in April of 1746, when a noted French scientist named Jean-Antoine Nollet had two hundred monks in Paris arrange themselves into a long line by instructing each of them to hold onto the end of a twenty-five foot iron wire. Once this mile-long human and iron chain was complete, Nollet then connected one end of the wire to a primitive battery and sent an electric shock along the line (Standage, 1999). This eighteenth-century experiment was the first of many tests of the theory that electricity could be harnessed to send a message via wire over great distances. The shock received by each of the monks was literally telegraphed from one end of the wire to the other.

The term telegraphy was coined nearly fifty years later (1791) by Miot de Melito, a French classical scholar and friend of Claude Chappe, the founder of the first form of the telegraph, the optical telegraph. This form of the telegraph, which consisted of one long rotatable piece of steel with two smaller rotatable pieces of steel that were all controlled by an opera-

Chappe Telegraph (optical relay semaphore system): copy of a "Milan" Chappe tower from 1809. Courtesy of the Wikipedia Commons.

tor via a series of cables and pulleys, represented in itself an early form of communication literacy. Operators of these devices were highly specialized communicators who relied upon specific codebooks that allowed them to create optical symbols. The meanings of these symbols were virtually unknown to those who did not have access to the codes.

Chappe's friend and scholar Melito suggested the original term, telegraphe, or "far writer," and thus the term telegraph was born (Standage, 1999). By the middle of the nineteenth century, continued experimentation by many scientists—including such notables as Samuel F.B. Morse, who later became known as the Father of the Telegraph through his development of Morse Code—eventually led to the birth and widespread use of the electronic telegraph. In 1870, the inventor Thomas Edison, who himself was once a telegraph operator, used his knowledge of telegraphy to construct the Universal Stock Ticker, a device that was "the first mechanical means of conveying stock prices ('quotes') over long distance telegraph wiring" (News ticker, 2007).

Morse code, along with the stock abbreviations typed on ticker tapes, represented new multiliteracies during this time period. Electronic telegraph operators and readers of ticker tapes, like operators of optical telegraphs from the previous century, were familiar with codes that were unknown to many.

Thomas Edison. Photograph courtesy of the Library of Congress.

A modern form of the ticker tape, News Tickers, also known as crawlers, is a method in which the text is displayed, usually on the bottom tenth of television screens or on thin display boards that wrap around buildings, known as zippers. News tickers have their origins with Edison's Universal Stock Ticker because "the name 'ticker' comes from the paper ticker tape machines, which once printed news onto a moving tape" (News ticker, 2007).

The first use of a news ticker occurred during the initial broadcast of the National Broadcast Company's (NBC) *Today Show* during its debut on January 14th, 1952. This earliest form of news ticker consisted of typewritten headlines on a piece of paper placed at the bottom of the camera, and because of lack of popularity, it was dropped shortly thereafter (News ticker, 2007).

Within three decades, however, many local television stations in northern areas of the United States used recent technological advances to supply viewers with current weather events and related school closings. The terrorist attacks of September 11, 2001 created a boom in news tickers, and now virtually all major news channels use this type of digital, scrolling media display. One of the most prevalent forms of streaming messages today, news tickers can be viewed through multiple electronic devices, such as televisions, computers and Personal Data Assistants (PDAs). This form of textual communication, such as CNBC Ticker, is a computer simulation of ticker tapes that stream across the bottom of the screen, and "shows security and index symbols just like the old ticker tapes that received information by telegraph, but unlike those ticker tapes, it is digital" (CNBC Ticker, 2007).

Because this crawling medium is prevalent in many commonly used electronic devices and displays data usually comprised of symbols and abbreviations that are specific to a certain industry or occupation (i.e., stock market jargon), streaming messages is an important form of an alternative postmodern literacy. For those individuals who cannot read or who are not familiar with the meanings behind the symbols in streaming messages, the lack of comprehension represents an inability to negotiate or interact with potentially important forms of information.

Streaming messages like the ones found on television screens also add a new dimension to textuality by dividing the attention of the reader. Essentially, there is the main text of the program being watched and a secondary or subtext that runs beneath. In this manner, the attention of the reader is moved from the primary text—that is, the main program being watched—to a secondary text. As a result, this new multiliteracy changes the type of reading being employed in a distinctly postmodern manner. Today, students are more accustomed to dividing their attention among multiple text and graphical sources.

17

Hmong Story Cloths

Lisa Repaskey

Traditional Hmong Story Cloth. Photograph by Beavela.

Multiliteracies: Beyond Text and the Written Word, pages 77–82

As the Vietnam War was coming to an end in 1975, the Americans and their allies were racing to flee the country and the newly formed Communist Government. The Hmong people, who lived high in the mountains of Laos, had been strong allies of the U.S. during the war and were recruited by the CIA to help fight the communists. Once the war came to an abrupt end, the Hmong people were in grave danger of being slaughtered by the North Vietnamese-backed Pathet Lao government because of their close involvement with the Americans (Cha, 1996). The lucky ones were able to escape the coming brutality along with the Americans. For the majority of Hmong, the route to escape wasn't as easy. The people were marked for genocide, but fleeing their homeland was a difficult proposition (Cha, 1996). Chemical and biological weapons were inflicted upon them. Those who were able to escape had to trek through mountainous jungles and cross the treacherous Mekong River where they ended up living in refugee camps in neighboring Thailand (Lindsay, n.d.).

The Hmong are ethnically Chinese. In the 1800s, the Hmong people, which means "free people," were forced from their homes in China, finding refuge in the mountains of Laos, Thailand, Cambodia, and Vietnam, of what was then French Indochina. Agrarian people who grew crops and raised livestock, the Hmong chose to live high in the mountains where they could maintain their ancient traditions and live in freedom (Dao, n.d.).

Needlework and arts are important in Hmong culture. Traditional clothing for New Year's celebrations, marriages, births, and other important events, as well as everyday use, are an important part of the Hmong cultural identity. Particularly distinctive is the tradition of brightly colored needlework on black fabric, also known as paj ntaub (pronounced "pa ndow) or "flower cloth" (Breneman, 2005). The intricate detail of this form of traditional needlepoint has been an integral part of the Hmong traditions for thousands of years. Life in the harsh refugee camps of Thailand helped to transform the paj ntaub into a pictorial representation of the often brutal realities of fleeing one's homeland and the day-to-day squalor and precarious existence of life in the refugee camps (Peterson, 1988).

Much like the Winter Count Drawings of the Plains tribes in North America, the paj ntaub became a means for the Hmong people to save their histories and share them with succeeding generations. These "story cloths" tell the horrifying stories of fleeing a brutal communist regime that was bent on destroying a people who had sided with the American government during the Vietnam War, as well as what life was like during the escape to the refugee camps and life in the refugee camps themselves.

Hmong Story Cloth, 2007. Courtesy of Susan Seater.

The strong narrative tradition of the Hmong people, along with their artistic needlework skill, helped to transform the paj ntuab into "story cloths," a powerful form of alternative literacy (Cha, 1996). Through the medium of an old tradition, the modern story of Hmong history and culture is told. Interestingly enough, this creation of a new and highly unique form of literacy came about for financial reasons. The Hmong needed to provide income for their families in the Thai refugee camps, and this centuries-old skill of intricate needlework was a viable means by which skilled embroiderers could provide income for their families.

An interesting synergism evolved in the camps that led to the creation of the paj ntaub from the traditional "flower cloths" into the modern "story cloths." Living in the refugee camps, the Hmong had little to do, having lost their homes back in the mountains of Laos. Women continued to do their needlework. The men, who had been taught to illustrate the school primers that the missionaries created in the 1960s to capture traditional Hmong folk tales, continued to draw. The men's drawings and the women's needlepoint merged when the women decided to see if they could capture

Hmong Story Cloth, 2007. Courtesy of Susan Seater.

these illustrations onto the paj ntaub (Guensburg, 1996). The illustrations on the traditional paj ntaub fabric were created by the men, who sketched these "stories" completely freehand with no model on which to base their illustrations. When the illustrations were completed onto the paj ntaub, the women completed the intricate details of the needlework without anything to guide them except their own keen eyesight. Because of the extraordinarily rich details of the paj ntaub, it can take up to several months to complete one story cloth (Cha, 1996).

The aid workers from around the world who worked with the Hmong refugees in the Thai camps were so impressed with the incredible beauty of these paj ntaubs that they began purchasing them from the Hmong and shipping them home to their families and friends. As the Hmong people have been resettled around the world, many have come to make a new life in the United States. Over 180,000 Hmong now live in the United States, although the largest concentrations of Hmong are in Minnesota, Wiscon-

Hmong Story Cloth, 2007. Courtesy of Susan Seater.

sin, and areas around Fresno, California where they have chosen to settle and begin their new lives (Lindsay, n.d.). Hmong story cloths continue to be made and sold, this time in local flea markets, by word of mouth, and even on eBay to people who want to own a piece of this incredibly powerful narrative history.

Out of economic necessity, a new form of literacy was created. These story cloths, based from the traditional paj ntaub, or "flower cloth," became a narrative, pictorial textile art, born from the strong oral tradition of the Hmong people that depicts the history, culture, and daily lives of its people (Peterson, 1988). These story cloths also record the challenges, battles, and loss of life that occurred as the Hmong were forced to flee Laos (Peterson, 1988). This new literacy of story cloths, re-established out of necessity and merged with the strong oral traditions of the Hmong people, are important texts that show the group's cultural identification, intercultural communication, collective actions, and history (Peterson, 1988). As such, Hmong story clothes represent a particularly interesting example of an alternative literacy—one with distinctly postmodern overtones of communication, economics, and political struggle.

18

The Power of Puppetry

Jennifer Diptee

Marionette puppets. Photograph by Miriam Lipsky.

Multiliteracies: Beyond Text and the Written Word, pages 83–87

The oral tradition of the marionette or puppet is an art form that can be found in many cultures and has historically emerged as one that speaks to and for the people. Whether the goal was to preach morality, protest social injustice, change public opinion, or carry hidden messages to and from the repressed, puppetry held more purpose than just entertainment. This oral and visual art form served as a communication tool and attempted to influence, explain, and teach audiences about the social, political, and religious issues of their time. Through a language of gestures, words, song, dance, emotions, and ideals, puppetry can be interpreted as an ancient and unique form of literacy.

Traditional forms of puppetry and marionette performance can be traced as far back to the ancient Greeks, where writings of Xenophon around 422 B.C. reveal evidence of the lost art. Literature from Aristotle, Archimedes, Plato, and Herodotus are infused with references to *neurospasta*, which meant "string-pulling" that controlled heads, hands, eyes, shoulders, and legs. Jointed, string-operated figures of wood were even found in ancient Egyptian graves circa 2000 B.C. where historians believed they were used as a medium for displaying rituals and ceremonies. In England during the 15th century, puritans used puppets as a service to the church, where Bible stories that spread morality could be performed. Puppeteers in Burma not only used puppetry to communicate messages between common folk, but as a way for commoners to communicate messages to the king, as members of the court would decipher the codes during the shows. During the early 17th century, a famous puppet named Karagiozis (found in both Greece and Turkey) served as a live news service for the folk, extending gossip of the day as well as creating parodies and satires out of local events and government. Europe's use of puppets to reveal dissent and revolutionary propaganda among the public drew such crowds to the streets that governments eventually condemned puppetry as "criminal" and banned such displays in public. Regardless of time period or culture, the general pattern suggests that puppets were oral traditions that utilized mass communication as a means of expression, education, and entertainment for the disenfranchised (Mogg, 2000).

Interestingly, one of history's more notable puppet characters was Punch, who emerged out of the political turmoil during the 17th century in England. Derived from the Italian commedia dell'arte figure Pulcinella, Punch and his wife Judy (his female equivalent) were voices of dissent among the commoners against the bourgeois. Characterized as a hunchbacked, obese, and lazy trickster armed with raw and brutal satire, Punch critiqued rules, lawmakers, ideals, morals, and God, and even tricked Death by avoiding hanging during his outrageous acts. He was considered a hero by the people, who stood for "freedom both of act and speech" and was an "enthusiastic championship of the poor and oppressed" (Spielmann, 1985, p. 100). Punch understood the people's plight and in turn armed them with knowledge—the knowledge that an unhappy society that required change (Spielmann, 1895; Janik & Nelson, 1998).

In contemporary culture, the significance of puppetry as a form of literacy can be best described in the more recent movement called political, radical, or protest puppetry that began in the 1960s as a result of the social upheaval of the time. This subversive political role began with the work of Peter Schumann, who founded the Bread and Puppet Theatre in 1962. The thought behind the movement was that since theatre was common, it was the perfect arena to spread messages to the masses without sounding educational or didactic. The first production's focus was on police presence, as that was a pressing issue of the time. The Bread and Puppet Theatre later made its mark by protesting against the American involvement in the Vietnam War and opposing the army draft and the World Trade Organization (Mogg, 2000).

The important aspect that makes political puppets and radical puppetry more than just entertainment, but rather a form of literacy, is that by deciphering the important messages spread by the puppet theatres, audiences were provided an empowerment and a social awareness of their environment. This political literacy held a powerful influence on how people

The Boss

"The Boss." A political statement through puppets. Published in: "What's the Matter with America" by William Allen White, *Collier's* magazine. Photograph courtesy of the Library of Congress.

critically viewed the issues around them. Those who could decipher the covert, and sometimes overt, messages had the power to make decisions, make choices, and make changes in society, ultimately regaining one's freedom. The best part about puppetry is that it reached everyone, from the wealthy, upper-class professionals to the lowly factory workers and illiterate immigrants, creating a sort of equality in communication. The more you were empowered with knowledge, the more you could become free (Mac Phee & Reuland, 2007).

Take, for instance, the string puppetry performances in India, where the Sangeet Natak Academy, the Punjab Arts Council, and the government of India wanted to boost its popularity among the new generation in Punjab. The purpose of the Academy was to educate the public and spread messages in villages and towns with low literacy rates. The tradition of string puppetry, termed Gopa Leela, in Orissa, India revolves around religious stories accompanied by devotional poetry (i.e., Lord Krishna's childhood life) so that the townsfolk gather and understand the messages. Similarly, in Bangladesh, activists such as Mustafa Monwar, known as the "puppet man," use puppets to spread social messages throughout a country known to hold extremely low literacy (considered as traditional reading/writing) rates. Through a weekly children's program that has been in operation since 1965, Monwar has delivered important messages including tolerance, preventing AIDS, child education and development, and living in harmony with nature.

The significance of puppetry as a literacy and as a means of social change can be seen in the establishment of numerous foundations and organizations across the world. Notably, the North American Center of Union Internationale de la Marionnette (UNIMA–USA), founded in 1966, is an organization where people volunteer and unite in order to promote inter-

Puppets. Photograph by Miriam Lipsky.

national appreciation and friendship regardless of race, political ideology, or religion through the use of puppetry.

In summary, puppetry is more than a means of communication; it is a type of literacy that enables the public to critique and voice their opinions about society. Being able to appreciate the meanings behind puppetry not only provides entertainment, but it can increase the public's awareness and ultimately provide knowledge as power to make decisions. For this reason, puppetry is not just a traditional art form but it also encompasses a unique expression of literacy that can be decoded and interpreted and used to educate societies worldwide.

19

Death T-Shirts

Yvonne D. Perry

Death T Shirt Commemorating the Life of Stack Bundles.

Multiliteracies: Beyond Text and the Written Word, pages 89–90

Historically, rituals honoring the dead have taken on various forms. In the 17th century before European contact, many artisans in Africa created funerary terra cottas to honor the dead, and these were kept in the homes of relatives after the death of a loved one. In addition, the dead were also honored through libations, or the ritual act of pouring a liquid offering on the ground. According to Visoná (2005) these fired clay images of humans once crafted by Lagoon artisans from the Côte d'Ivoire have been replaced by cement tombs, framed photographs, and memorial t-shirts.

Interestingly, in modern culture, one form of honoring the dead is through the creation of memorial t-shirts. This practice began with descendants of the African continent as a way to honor their dead (Shreve, 2007), employing this alternative literacy to give respect to lost family members and friends. According to Jean Shreve, the practice has its roots in the gangster culture of the west coast of the United States, where creating memorial t-shirts was a way to remember dead gang members in the 1990s and became especially popular when rapper Tupac Shakur's image was plastered on tees after his death. The practice gained further popularity with urban minorities and teenagers, and after 9/11, the general population embraced the practice as a way to give tribute to the dead ("Will It Ever Change," 2006).

Though illegitimate in many of their practices, gangs use memorial t-shirts to legitimize members of their group. This use of literacy is illuminated in light of what Szwed (2001) calls the social meaning of literacy. In his *Ethonography of Literacy*, he proposes that we focus on the roles that reading and writing play in the social life of participants, the contexts of their performances, and the way these are interpreted by ordinary people in the carrying out of ordinary activities (Heath, 1978). In this way, we see the meaning and structure of literacy outside the normal context of traditional textual forms. Considering its roots, some may consider it intriguing that this practice has "crossed over" to mainstream culture. Perhaps, however, this transition can be explained in the notion that honoring the dead appeals to many segments of the population.

The wearing of memorial t-shirts can also be characterized as a literacy event as defined by Heath (1978): "A literacy event is any occasion in which a piece of writing is integral to the nature of participants' interactions and their interpretive processes" (p. 445). These t-shirts with their graphical and textual formats allow the creators to express grief and remembrance in non-traditional ways. The wearers of these tees have found an innovative approach to interpreting the grieving process. Memorial t-shirts represent postmodernism by erasing boundaries and exploring alternative means of self-expression.

20

Roadside Memorials

Yvonne Perry

A roadside moral for Michael J. Ramirez on U.S. 1 in Coral Gables, Florida. Photograph by Eugene F. Provenzo, Jr.

Multiliteracies: Beyond Text and the Written Word, pages 91–95

The association of writing with memorials to the dead dates back to Ancient Egypt. Tombs dating from before 3,000 B.C. include examples of hieroglyphic text. In our era, we are creating similar representations in the form of roadside memorials. The creation of these memorials has proliferated in recent years. What do they tell us about the representation of death in American culture, and how are they related to larger issues of literacy found in the culture?

Roadside memorials represent a unique narrative form. A tragic scene on the side of a highway is transformed into a venue for sharing details about the life of a loved one. In this society where we have sanitized death in hospitals and nursing homes, this new form of literacy allows the grief stricken to communicate their sorrow to the world. In doing so, the creators of these memorials have brought death, and the way we mourn, out of the closet, and into the mainstream thought of American life. There is not a large body of scholarly work on roadside memorials, although a few studies do provide some insight on this distinctly postmodern means of grieving.

Roadside memorials allow families and loved ones who've encountered unbelievable heartache and tragedy to communicate their sorrow in a very public, yet essentially personal manner. Roadside memorials in the United States almost certainly have their origins in Hispanic tradition. The practice

Flowers left at a roadside moral for Michael J. Ramirez on U.S. 1 in Coral Gables, Florida. Photograph by Eugene F. Provenzo, Jr.

of erecting *descansos,* which are small remembrances placed at the scenes of untimely death, seems to have made its way into American culture as the Hispanic population in the United States has increased (Clark & Franzmann, 2006). Facilitating the trend were public outpourings of love such as those demonstrated by mourners leaving flowers at the gates of Buckingham Palace when Princess Diana died and similarly at the site of the World Trade Center attack of 9/11 (Collins & Rhine, 2003). Some believe that government-sponsored memorials such as the one erected in honor of soldiers who died in the Vietnam War on the mall in Washington, DC may have also precipitated the practice, acceptance, and healing power associated with public display and acknowledgement of grief (Clark & Franzmann, 2006). It is a common practice for people to leave token objects and representations of those memorialized beneath their names on the Vietnam Memorial wall.

Roadside memorials take on many forms. Typically, they are small white crosses with fresh or plastic flower arrangements. Many times they are fences or structures on the side of roadways that become "message boards" in memory of the deceased. People attach various mementos honoring the person's life—candles, teddy bears, pictures, notes, poems, pieces of clothing, balloons, ribbons, and the like. They have a communicative effect in that

Photographs and personal items of clothing left at a roadside memorial for Michael J. Ramirez on U.S. 1 in Coral Gables, Florida. Photograph by Eugene F. Provenzo, Jr.

they relay information about the victim. The deceased's date of birth, date of death (Clark & Franzmann, 2006), hobbies, organizational affiliations, and so on are often included. They tell a story about the memorialized person's life. These markers serve not only as remembrances of the dead but admonitions to the living, as in the case of signs warning against drunk driving.

Why do people feel the need to express grief in this immensely public way? Theories abound. One strongly held assumption suggests that mourners feel that the place where their loved one departed this earth is sacred. As Brian Doyle explains, "We know why we do this. We cannot *not* do this. We mark the spot where the soul left the body and returned to the Sender. These places are holy. They are holes wrenched open suddenly, often in flame, doors through which a soul has passed from this world" (Reid & Reid, 2001, p. 350). Others take a non-religious stance, believing that traditional ways of mourning are outdated, and hold little meaning in this time in our history (Doyle, 2004). In this context, traditional forms of mourning such as funerals and cemetery ceremonies do not adequately satisfy the need for meaningful expression of grief. According to Peter Read, cemeteries are too ordered and restrained; they have too many regulations. In contrast, roadside memorials allow mourners freedom to articulate grief as they see fit (Clark & Franzmann, 2006). In this respect, roadside memorials give "voice" to those who find the need to express themselves in less conventional ways. In doing so, they provide an alternative narrative space to the traditional funeral home, cemetery, or church. Creating these memorials allows grief-stricken families who had no control over the sudden, untimely death of their loved ones a measure of control in the manner in which they express their grief.

With an estimated 4,000 to 8,000 new memorials being constructed each year, many states have begun to impose restrictions and regulations on the practice (Zaslow, 2005). Some states have designed and made available uniform, non-sectarian markers to be used. These signs can cost from one hundred to one-thousand dollars and are often paid for by the family of the victim or a sponsor. In rare cases, a municipality will pay the costs. In addition to various size limitations some states impose, others have regulations about the amount of time these memorials may remain up. In Thousand Oaks, California, memorials are only allowed to remain in place for 30 days. In Atlantic City, New Jersey, they may only stand for 10 days (Hughes, 2002). Some states have prohibited the creation of roadside memorials altogether. However, once constructed, because of the sensitive nature of their meaning, government officials will not dismantle these memorials out of respect for the family.

This new narrative form is not necessarily embraced by the general public. In fact, American roadways and expressways have always been filled with advertisements of every imaginable sort. We are encouraged to eat here, buy there, vacation here, think this, and vote that. This new mode of communication, however, is raising non-traditional questions about the free speech rights of mourners. Some say these memorials are distracting, while others say they are intrusive and generate unnecessary sadness for those who pass by them. Some compare them to graffiti, and say they are an eyesore, especially if they are neglected or fall into disrepair (Clark & Franzmann, 2006).

The following cases highlight this issue: In the first, a family's home faces a memorial where two teenagers died in an accident. Whenever friends and family pass, day or night, they honk their horns. Even though the family sympathizes with the loved ones of the victims, the constant honking of the horns is so disturbing that the family goes to town officials for help. Even though an agreement is reached to stop the horn honking, the presence of the memorial makes the children feel that ghosts live there. In the second case, a gentleman who lives near a memorial of a t-shirt wrapped around a tree said that "if everybody built memorials, trees would be covered, and there would be crosses everywhere" (Zaslow, 2005).

As a public display, narrative form, and new type of literate act, roadside memorials encourage debate. No matter what the opinion of people on the issue, it is clear that they represent an important cultural artifact. Many Americans have taken the mourning process out of their of houses of worship and the dark recesses of cemeteries, and into the streets in the form of highly personal and public remembrances of those they loved and lost in death.

21

Graffiti

Lisa Repaskey

Graffiti mecca in Long Island City, New York. Photograph by Cassidy Curtis.

According to Elizabeth Moje (2000), if theorists claim literacy as a tool that transforms thought and experience, then we also need to take a closer look at the unsanctioned literacy practices of margin-

Multiliteracies: Beyond Text and the Written Word, pages 97–99

alized adolescents in our society. We need to ask ourselves what these so-called unsanctioned literacy practices do for the lives of adolescents.

Graffiti is "markings, as initials, slogans, or drawings, written, spray-painted, or sketched on a sidewalk, wall of a building or public restroom, or the like" (Moje, 2000). Graffiti has always gotten a bad rap as being destructive and deviant because of its close association with gangs and gang life. Tagging is similar to graffiti, but is a distant and quite distinctive "cousin" with its own embedded rules and codes.

Thumbnail photos by Cassidy Curtis of Graffiti mecca in Long Island City, New York.

At first glance, the multicolored, spray-painted pictures, letters, and symbols scrawled across doors, walls, and highway overpasses hardly seem like they could be considered a legitimate form of literacy, especially when eagerly practiced by adolescents and other marginalized youth, referred to as "gangsta adolescents" by Moje (2000). Other forms of the alternative literacies embraced by these marginalized youth are "music, dress codes, make-up, tattoos, body movements, gestures, and hand signs." These are all highly visible symbols that help construct and shape the marginalized adolescents' identity and their use of literacy (Moje, 2000). In mainstream culture, these literacy practices are viewed as worrisome and deviant, with those who are engaging in them openly resisting traditional authority. Yet, if we are willing to lay down our biases and take a closer look at the forms of literacy that these marginalized adolescents are engaged in, we would discover an alternative literacy that is "a social practice... (that is deeply embedded) with its own rules and meaning surrounding it" (MacGillivray, 2007).

Graffiti art in particular can be a highly artistic representation. As a form of literacy it is of particular interest because it often incorporates artistic forms and representation with text. This is something vastly different than either an illustration of something or a textual description. Instead, it represents a unique synthesis.

These forms of adolescent self-expression give us insights on a number of unique levels. One is the idea that text may be linked in the minds of many individuals to something other than text. Such an approach suggests that traditional models of reading—specifically phonics—may be highly limited in terms of the realities of how adolescents function with text and image in the real world.

22

Patriotic Symbols

Gabriel Quintana

I Want You for the U.S. Army. Illustration by James Montgomery Flagg (1877–1960). Courtesy of the Library of Congress.

Multiliteracies: Beyond Text and the Written Word, pages 101–105

Patriotic symbols represent a language system with clear associations and meanings. Decoding these meanings involves a significant, yet often overlooked type of literacy. Images of the American flag, a bald eagle, the Liberty Bell, Uncle Sam, and the Statue of Liberty all evoke specific associations. They provide a common language that binds a people together, even though quite often their precise understanding of these symbols is not the same.

Patriotic symbols have evolved over the course of time. They did not simply appear at the time of the American Revolution, but rather, they took seed, grew, and evolved. Eugene F. Provenzo, Jr. (1984), for example, in his article "Education and the Iconography of the Republic," shows how the figure of Liberty was gradually introduced over a 100-year period into the consciousness of American children—only achieving the status it has today in the consciousness of the country's citizens by the time of the Civil War.

Why do Americans associate the objects in the preceding list as being patriotic? Why do they associate the Statue of Liberty with the pursuit of freedom, the flag with unity, the eagle with heroism and the defense of our nation? In terms of physical reality, the Statue of Liberty is no more than a large copper, oxidizing sculpture. The flag is simply a piece of cloth fluttering in the wind. The bald eagle is arguably one of the uglier and more rapa-

Liberty Bell in Independence Hall, Philadelphia, PA. Courtesy of the Library of Congress.

American eagle as a patriotic symbol. Courtesy of the Library of Congress.

cious birds of the North American continent. It was rejected by Benjamin Franklin, who advocated for the turkey, a bird he considered considerably more respectable and solid as a symbolic representation of the new nation (MacArthur, 2008).

How do people learn about these symbols? Essentially, we come to understand their meaning—we become literate about them—through a constant process of association and representation. Eagles and the flag are repeated as symbols on the pages of the comic books we read as children; the colors of red, white, and blue come to be associated with holidays such as the Fourth of July; we see the eagle on the staff that holds the flag in our nation's courtrooms and classrooms.

The symbols of American patriotism rarely developed by chance. Each patriotic symbol has its historical roots. Take the American flag for instance. After the Declaration of Independence was signed on July 4, 1776, the development of an American identity became crucial. What would show independence from Great Britain and continuity with our English history? It is no accident that the American flag has the same colors as the British Union Jack, or that it strikes out with new symbols—stars—to represent the loose configuration of semi-autonomous states that made up the United States of America (Adams, 2007).

Each patriotic symbol contributes to a complex and interrelated vocabulary that citizens learn through an almost automatic process of becoming Americans. Sometimes this process of "Americanization" is conscious, as in the recital of the Pledge of Allegiance to the Flag. The Pledge, which

Pledge of allegiance to the flag, 8th Division (Washington, D.C.). Frances Benjamin Johnston, Photographer, c. 1899. Courtesy of the Library of Congress.

was written in the early 1890s by the children's magazine editor Francis J. Bellamy, was consciously created in order to inspire patriotism among public school children (Baer, 1992). Targeting recently arrived immigrant children, it deliberately created a knowledge base and set of associations with the nation's flag—a flag that symbolically represented the country the children were a part of (Baer, 1992).

Patriotic symbols as a type of literacy operate in a number of different ways. These include their function as concrete objects that an individual can see and touch such as the flag, the Liberty Bell, or the Lincoln Memorial. Other symbols take on their meaning through historical association. Thus, a specific event such as the raising of the American flag at Iwo Jima's Mount Suribachi during World War II represents the creation of a patriotic symbol that is part of a historical representation—that is, the photograph of the flag being raised—an event staged by the photographer after the event (Ross, 1985).

Interestingly, concrete objects that are patriotic symbols become merged with historical associations. Thus in the case of the flag raising at Iwo Jima, not only is the flag represented as patriotic symbol, but the actual event that includes the flag also becomes a symbol in and of itself.

American Marines raising American flag on Mount Suribachi, Iwo Jima. Gelatin silver print, 1945. Photograph by Joe Rosenthal. Courtesy of the Library of Congress.

In conclusion, if literacy is, as the Oxford dictionary says, "competence or knowledge in a specified area," then patriotic symbols must be understood as a complex form of literacy—one of the multiliteracies in which we are interested in this work. Understanding such literacies and their role in creating a national consciousness is yet one additional dimension of the complex and interwoven phenomenon we understand as shaping and defining our national identity.

23

Baby Sign Language

Yvonne Perry

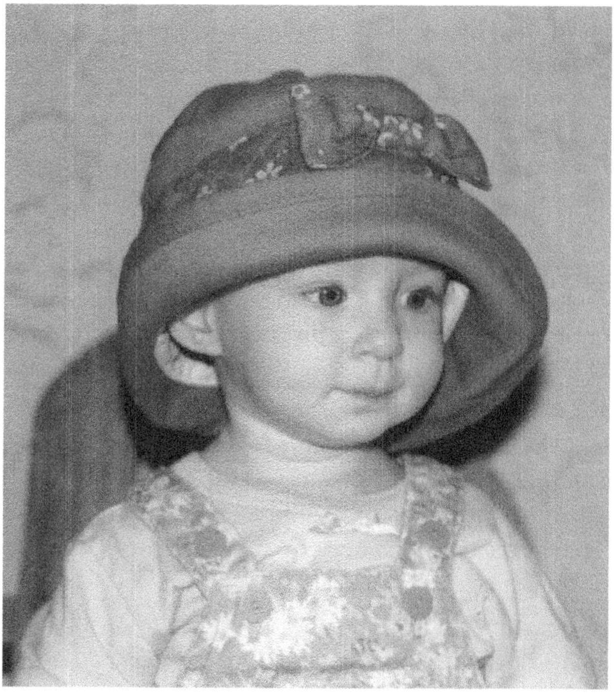

"Room to Grow." Photo by Miriam Lipsky.

Multiliteracies: Beyond Text and the Written Word, pages 107–110

At one time in our history, children were admonished to be seen and not heard. Today, children have been elevated in our society to the point where we not only want to see and hear them, but we also want to communicate with them and have insight into what they are thinking and feeling as early as infancy. Hence the birth of a new literacy called *baby sign language*. Seemingly, in this age of speed and impatience, we have become weary of waiting two years for babies to acquire language. Goodwyn, Acredolo, and Brown (2000) said that between ten months and two years of age, children and parents become frustrated with the slowness of the process of language acquisition. Based on their gesturing and whining, children have the desire to speak to us, but lack the fine motor coordination to do so. As a result, many parents are using a baby sign language to communicate with their babies.

This new form of literacy is groundbreaking because the door has been opened in the area of infant literacy. How many times have you looked at an infant and wondered what they were thinking? Since the beginning of time, mothers and fathers have been engaged in a trial and error system to identify the wants and needs of their babies. As any parent can attest, not knowing why a baby wakes up crying at two in the morning can be exasperating. Baby sign language can bring an end to the guessing games. In their research, Goodwyn, Acredolo, and Brown (2000) noted the following experience: A 16-month-old who awoke crying in the night was able to point and use his "afraid" gesture (patting on his chest) to let his mother know he was afraid of the clown doll on his dresser. Without the gesture, she might have put the doll in bed with him!

The foundation for this new literacy was established by research on symbol formation conducted by Werner and Kaplan (1963). They introduced the idea that in order for a child to acquire an ability to represent thoughts and objects, he or she must be able to create distance between the symbol and the object.

Drs. Acredolo and Goodwyn, the leaders in the area of baby signing, and other researchers extended Werner and Kaplan's idea and began to look at gestures. At about 10 months of age, babies begin to use a small group of gestures indicating that they are ready to begin the communication process. It is at this point that Dr. Acredolo and Dr. Goodwyn advocate using gestures, or "simple physical actions" to represent objects and events. Some of these gestures include those illustrated in Table 23.1 (Goodwyn et al., 2000).

Incorporating this method seems to be a natural progression in the development of children. According to Critchley (1970), children use over 150 natural gestures and signs, many of which they unlearn or modify as

Object/Event	Gesture
Drink	Thumb to Mouth
More	Index Fingers Tapping
Where?	Palms Up

they grow older, and Acredolo and Goodwyn (1993) stated that children can more easily manage gestures than words. In order to develop a set of gestures to use in communicating, parents are encouraged to use the gestures in tandem with word repetition. Parents may use their own gestures or ones suggested by the various authors of programs currently on the market. Some researchers advocate using standard American Sign Language. This, however, would require significant training since American Sign Language (ASL) is a complex gestural language. For parents of hearing children, this may not be feasible.

Even though those parents who use baby signing sing its praises, questions have arisen. Will this cause a delay in language acquisition? Studies have shown that it does not. In fact, there is evidence to suggest that children who are trained to use baby sign language outperform their peers in vocabulary

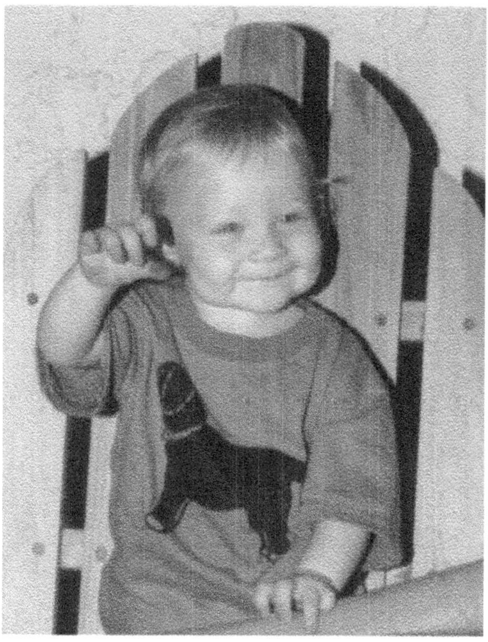

This baby is making the sign for "milk." Photo by Miriam Lipsky.

development (Goodwyn et al., 2000). Evidence from longitudinal studies also indicates that the effects of being trained in baby sign language last into second grade, where students who learned signing as babies were scoring 12 points higher on a measure of IQ (Acredolo & Goodwyn, 2000).

What are the implications for this emerging literacy? With the explosion of books, videos, and training kits on the subject, we are sure to see this new form of literacy in use by those parents who are looking for yet another way to speed up an otherwise slow process. In this age of high-speed internet, instant and text messaging, who has the time to wait for children to learn the intricacies of the spoken word? Baby signing speeds up the process and eliminates some of the frustration.

24

The Human Genome Project as Literacy

Kathryn LeRoy

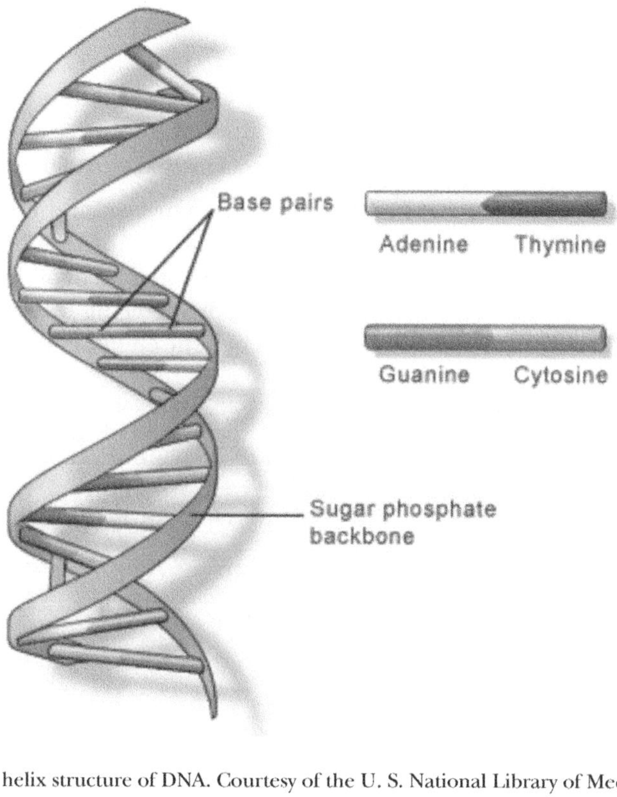

The double helix structure of DNA. Courtesy of the U. S. National Library of Medicine.

Multiliteracies: Beyond Text and the Written Word, pages 111–114

Watson and Crick changed for all time the meaning of scientific literacy. In no previous time in history has it been more important than today for Americans to be scientifically literate. Based on the work of Watson, Crick, and others, the Human Genome Project was established as a worldwide research effort that includes the mapping of the structure of human DNA and determining the location of an estimated 20,000 to 25,000 human genes.

What is a genome anyway? A genome is the entire set of genetic information of an organism including DNA and RNA. It holds all the information for making a complete individual. Each person's specific genome contains the genes that carry the information for determining how that person will look and sometimes even how they will behave. DNA is made up of four substances called nucleotides. Each nucleotide contains a different base: adenine (A), guanine (G), cytosine (C) or thymine (T). The entire genomic alphabet is made up of only four letters—A, T, C, and G. It can become very difficult to decipher the language of DNA as these letters are repeated millions or billions of times within a gene. It is the specific sequence of the letters (nucleotides) that make up the language (Baker, 1996).

The information generated from the Human Genome Project is expected to be the roadmap for biomedical science in the 21st century and beyond. This emergent knowledge will lead to the treatment of thousands of genetic diseases that afflict mankind with medicine being forever changed as new technologies applied to agricultural genetic engineering will appear.

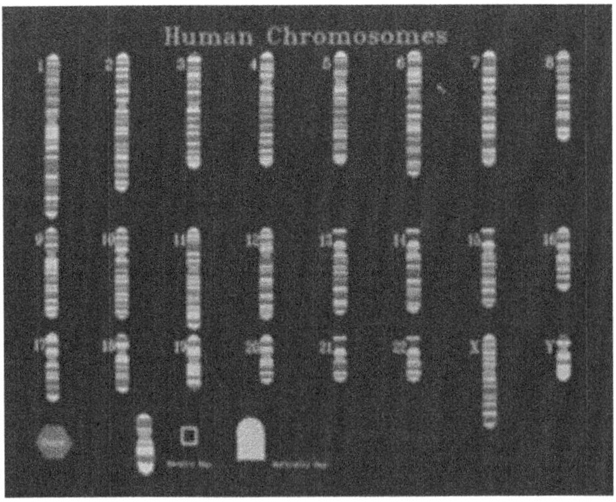

Human chromosomes. Courtesy of The Human Genome Project.

The ability to clone exact matches of high producing plants and animals and the production of bio-fuels will leave the realm of science fiction and enter into reality.

You can think of the Human Genome Project as a highway map of the human genome, just as there are road maps, geographical maps, and topographical maps of specific locations, there are different genomic maps that describe specific locations of genes on DNA. The Human Genome Project Information web site (2007a) states that this rapidly emerging science will soon infiltrate all aspects of society with endless possibilities for uses of this biological research, but at the same time require reflection and pause on the social, political, and ethical implications. With these implications comes a necessary literacy that is mandatory of every member of society so that ethical judgments can be made as this science pushes forward. Shortly, not only will the genetic causes of many diseases including sickle cell anemia, Tay-Sachs disease, cystic fibrosis, and many forms of cancer become known, but one will be able to identify these diseases before they occur in an individual. This surely could threaten one's right to privacy or create larger societal issues due to new reproductive technologies.

Another aspect is the controversy over genetically modified (GM) food. GM food's DNA is altered by a technology called genetic engineering. This technology allows for the incorporation of DNA from one species to be joined with the DNA of another species thus forming a transgenic species. Recently, about 167 million acres grown by over 7 million farmers in 18 countries were planted with transgenic crops, including herbicide- and insecticide-resistant soybeans, corn, cotton, and canola. Other crops grown commercially could end hunger in poor nations: genetically engineered rice with increased iron and vitamins may alleviate chronic malnutrition in Asian countries, and a variety of plants are able to survive weather extremes, according to the Human Genome Project web site (2007b). With these discoveries come ethical, legal, and societal questions. For example, what impact may these new "species" have on human health? Or is it ethical to tamper with the natural order of life? Or can a patent be issued to a living organism? These and other questions, remain unanswered on today's horizon.

The American Association for the Advancement of Science (AAAS) believes science literacy and the public understanding of science is crucial to protect the rights of members of society and has made a commitment to produce documents to further literacy on this emerging science. Such publications as *Your Genes, Your Choices: Exploring the Issues Raised by Genetic Research* (AAAS, 1999) provide the public straightforward scenarios that describe the potential uses of genetic engineering and what issues should be considered as this field expands.

With the dawn of the 21st century, man has inherited the responsibility to protect his world. This can only be accomplished through scientific literacy.

25

Fashion Branding

Yvonne Perry

Illustration in: Demorest's family magazine, December, 1889, p. 124. Courtesy of the Library of Congress.

Multiliteracies: Beyond Text and the Written Word, pages 115–118

In an article in the December, 1842 edition of *Lady's World of Fashion* magazine, one finds rich descriptions of the styles of the day—an underdress of Pekin silk, over which is worn a mantilla of violet velvet; a robe de chambre, made of a rich blue cachemire. Among the pages of vivid, detailed descriptions of fabrics, ribbons, bows, and trim, there isn't any mention of a brand or designer label.

If you thumb though a magazine today, you'll see a plethora of brands and designer labels attached to various photographic images. A brand is loosely defined as a set of pictures, symbols and/or concepts that represent a product. Brands or labels may refer to names, slogans, designs, shapes, patterns, and so on. These portraits are literary in nature because like written text, they convey messages to their "readers." These messages, however, don't require a degree of skill in "deciphering the code" as reading does. All one needs to do is be a fan of popular culture. One becomes literate in this area by watching television, perusing magazines, watching music videos, and keeping abreast of the trends in New York, Paris, and London. The messages sent are created by "authors" of sorts, who speak very powerfully to the human psyche, sometimes without uttering a word.

Fashion branding is a highly researched, carefully and cunningly created phenomenon designed to stimulate a positive response toward a particular brand of clothing. What do you think of when you see an image of an alligator on a shirt? What about a gentleman playing polo? The manufacturers are selling the lifestyle being portrayed by these articles of clothing and have expended large amounts of money to entice you into believing that if you buy their products, you will live the life of the people in their advertisements. Perhaps what makes this literacy so insidious is the ease by which it elicits a response from the consumer. This tyranny of brands has a major impact on the values of our culture.

Researchers have determined that recognition of brands and labels may begin as young as two years of age (Ross & Harradine, 2004). Marketers believe the sooner you target consumers, the greater chance you have of building a loyal customer for life. At the onset, this is done in much the same way that a child acquires the tools of written and spoken discourse. A child understands the function of print through various levels of exposure to it.

Purcell-Gates (2001), in her research of literacy acquisition in the years prior to school instruction, developed a model entitled "The Dimensions of Written Language Knowledge Learned by Young Children Through Experience, and Constrained by Cultural Practice, Prior to Formal Instruction." She states that children tend to learn implicitly about written language in three dimensions, each of which limit and define the other. They begin at the outer dimension where everything they learn about language is determined by their "particular sociolinguistic communities and culture." In this dimension, they learn about written language formats, and the purpose of language (Purcell-Gates, 2001).

Similarly, branding plows a path into the minds of children; exposure to massive levels at early stages of the formative years increases awareness of the use and function of the various brands and labels to which they are exposed through television, especially by means of commercial advertisements. These advertisements act as instructors: The more they are viewed, the stronger the ability becomes to recall brands, thereby strengthening awareness, brand association, and image (Ross & Harradine, 2004). Children come to realize implicitly, just as in language development, that the symbols, images, designs, shapes, and so on have a function.

As children get older, they begin to associate these brands and labels with certain attitudes, emotions, and dispositions. The Nike "swoosh" for instance, evolves into more than a mere symbol. Ross and Harradine (2004) use Maslow's hierarchy to assert that children may no longer be motivated by base level physiological and safety needs—by wearing footwear simply to protect their feet—but by the need to belong to primary and secondary reference groups or by the need for self-esteem (the status levels that some brands portray).

Perhaps nowhere else is this trend more prevalent than with the teenage demographic. They are made brand conscious by virtually constant exposure to the internet, chat rooms, and MTV programming; Parker, Hermans, and Schaefer (2004) assert that the universal use of these forms of

Branding is no longer reserved for the front of shirts. Photograph by Miriam Lipsky.

The Hollister Corporation's brand symbol of the flying seagull, conveys a surfer/beach theme. Photograph by Miriam Lipsky.

media "homogenizes" teenagers' preferences. This constant reinforcement of brand label consciousness perpetuates the ideas and concepts associated with these products.

Unfortunately, what you wear speaks volumes in many adult, adolescent, and children's circles. Branding has given clothes, shoes, and accessories a voice, and for many, they identify the level of status or worth attributed to individuals. Brand labels say you are fashionable, youthful, energetic, wealthy, smart, reckless, cool, or any number of other qualities concocted by advertisers in their massive media campaigns.

26

Traffic Signs

William B. Deese

Roman milestone along the Apian Way. Photograph courtesy of Sasha Walton.

Multiliteracies: Beyond Text and the Written Word, pages 119–121

A symbol is defined as "a written character or mark used to represent something; a letter, figure, or sign conventionally standing for some object, process, etc." (Traffic signs, 2007). Traffic signs today are symbols that incorporate combinations of shapes, written text, and colors. These signs, which are used for a multitude of purposes, are largely dependent on national guidelines, although international organizations, such as the Vienna Convention on Road Signs, Signals of November 8, 1968, and the 1908 International Road Congress in Rome, have attempted to standardize them across political borders. The Vienna Convention determined that traffic signs are delineated into eight categories: danger warning signs; priority signs; prohibitory or restrictive signs; mandatory signs; special regulation signs; information, facilities, or service signs; direction, position, or indication signs; and additional panels (Traffic signs, 2007).

Modern-day traffic signs have their origins in early civilizations. Although not as detailed as many contemporary examples, early road signs nevertheless served important functions in their respective societies. The earliest known examples of road signs served as markers that assisted travelers in determining distance. Although constructed of different materials, in essence these roadside symbols were the equivalent of modern-day automobile mile markers.

As early civilizations became more and more advanced, the nature of the signs themselves changed. Road signs became more detailed, evolving from symbol-based forms to include textual forms of literacy. An example of this type of sign arose in Europe in the Middle Ages, when multidirectional signs at intersections became common (Traffic signs, 2007).

Because of the increase in international travel, modern traffic signs have shifted away from text-only forms toward symbols that are used to overcome

Multilingual road sign in Quebec, Canada. Courtesy of the Wikipedia Commons.

"Strada Deformata." This traffic sign warns of an uneven road. Courtesy of the Wikipedia Commons.

the difficulties that a lack of linguistic knowledge may represent. Although various attempts have been made to standardize traffic signs globally, many variations still exist. Some governments, in an attempt to overcome difficulties in meaning in linguistically diverse areas, have resorted to signs that use multiple languages.

Even with the lack of written language, the meanings of certain symbols are often confusing. Many of the variations of traffic signs that exist in different regions can be extremely confusing to the outsider who may not be familiar with these symbols.

Knowledge of traffic signs can save lives, and therefore understanding of this multiliteracy is vital. Because of this, traffic signs have recently experienced an evolution back to earlier forms. Symbols, rather than text, are the preferred mode of communication in an increasingly complex linguistic world. People today find themselves living in a global economy where international travel is more and more frequent. As governments and international organizations continue their attempts to standardize transportation messages through the use of these symbols, travelers will find it increasingly important to familiarize themselves with these forms of symbolic literacy.

27

Measurement Literacy

Sheree T. Sharpe

Kilometers	Miles
1	0.62
5	3.10
10	6.21
15	9.32
20	12.42
50	31.06
100	62.1
500	310.6
1,000	621.3

Conversion table from kilometers to miles.

To be literate in measurement is to have the ability to understand quantities. Measurement is an important form of literacy because it allows us to quantify objects. Measurement literacy is also an important part of today's society because we work daily with length, weight, and time. Because measurement is a daily part of our lives, we rarely pay attention to it.

Measurement is essentially anything that can be quantified. We use measurement to purchase gasoline by the gallon, food by the pound, and electricity by the kilowatt. We also use measurement to measure the amount of land a person owns, the passage of time, the distance between cities,

Multiliteracies: Beyond Text and the Written Word, pages 123–126

money by currency, energy by the joule, and temperature in degrees Fahrenheit (Beckmann, 2005). Measurement is also used for the assessment of attitudes, values and perception in surveys, or in the testing of individual aptitude. Even music is a type of measurement; it's the division of time by which melody and rhythm are regulated.

Measurement is, by definition, systematic. Each measurement can be reduced into a system of units. A system of measurement, whether it is length, weight, or time, is a collection of standardized units (Beckmann, 2005). In order to understand measurement in any given instance, one has to determine what is being measured and how it is being measured. The two main systems of measurement used today in the United States are the U.S. customary system of measurement and the metric system (also known as the international system of units, or the SI system) (Beckmann, 2005). The metric system is decimal systems of weights that follow a well-organized interval system. The U.S. customary system has an ordinal relationship. Conversion between the two systems is possible, but with varying degrees of accuracy.

Most products in the United States have their measurement in both metric and U.S. customary system. Have you ever watched the weather channel when they report six inches of rain or snow? If you are literate you will know what the meteorologist means by six inches of snow. What if the meteorologist had said that the river had risen and roads were flooded three feet high. Would you be able to drive home through the flooded roads? You would have to be literate in measurement to know. What if the meteorologist had said one meter or ten decimeters instead? Would you be able to convert it to inches or feet? This poses a problem for many Americans located outside the United Stated where the metric system is prevalent.

The importance of measurement was summarized by William Thomson (a.k.a. Lord Kelvin, 1824–1907) who wrote:

> When you can measure what you are speaking about, and express it in numbers, you know something about it; but when you cannot express it in numbers, your knowledge is of a meager and unsatisfactory kind; it may be the beginning of knowledge, but you have scarcely in your thoughts advanced to the state of science. (Bartlett, 1968)

Therefore, it is the ability to measure something, in order to be knowledgeable about that thing, which makes a person measurement literate. The word measurement comes from the Greek word "*metron*," leading to the scientific study of measurement being called *metrology*. Units of measurement were among the first tools invented by humans. Sometime in the 4th and 3rd millennia BC, the ancient people of Egypt, Mesopotamia, the

Hebrew dry measures, Hebrew liquid measures. Courtesy of the Library of Congress.

Indus Valley, and Elam (in Iran) seem to have created the earliest known uniform systems of weights and measures. Early Babylonian and Egyptian records as well as the Bible indicate that time was measured by the periods of the sun, moon, and other heavenly bodies. The 360 degrees found in a circle may have been related to a year of 360 days. To compare the capacities of containers in the past, they were filled with plant seeds which were then counted to measure volume. They also indicate that length was first measured with the forearm, hand, or finger. Often measurement was based on the dimensions of the human body. Some believe that the original measurement of the English foot was from King Henry I (History of measurement, 2008). In ancient Israel, and also the Bible, Hebrew measures were separated by whether something was either dry or liquid. Today, this would be whether we are talking about mass (kilogram or pound) or capacity (liter or quart).

Testing as a measurement is among the many tools teachers used in making decisions concerning student progress. The government and educators use measurement in schools to assess students' ability to read, write, and perform mathematics and science. Measurement is used every day, but many have trouble interpreting and converting among the most common measurement systems (metric vs. U.S. customary). What would happen if people in the U.S. were unable to convert to the metric system? Would we be able to communicate with the world? As we become a more international and global culture, it is no longer enough to have measurement literacy in only the U.S. customary system; we must develop literacy in the metric system as well.

28

The Language of Dance

Jennifer Diptee

A young ballerina gets ready for her first recital. Photograph by Miriam Lipsky.

Multiliteracies: Beyond Text and the Written Word, pages 127–130

Until recently, research on literacy has focused on the reading and writing of printed texts. However, with the advent of digital and multimedia technologies, this approach to understanding literacy is no longer adequate. Increasingly, verbal and kinesthetic behaviors need to be included in our understanding of what it is to be literate. As part of an emerging awareness of multiliteracies, many literacy theorists believe a more pluralistic view of literacy needs to be developed—one that includes the ability to comprehend, interpret, analyze, respond, and interact with a growing variety of data sources (Sensenbaugh, 1990). Spatial and kinesthetic expressions should be a part of this new literacy, and should include the movements found in dance. These movements can be captured in dance notation, which is an evolving form of literacy—one shaped by both historical and contemporary technologies.

Similar to traditional texts, the language of dance is one which contains vocabulary, form, structure, choreography, style, function and notation distinct to individual types of dance. Ballet, ballroom, contemporary, folk, and jazz are but a few of the different types of dance which require a specific knowledge base and skills for execution. Informal dance forms may not require such a knowledge base, but those that are formal and skill-oriented demand a certain bodily and cognitive intelligence.

Take, for instance, classical ballet, which comprises various techniques, methods, and training dependent on which school (Russian, French, or Italian) it belongs to; includes distinctive rules of movement; and has its own vocabulary. An understanding of terminology such as grand plié, pirouette, barre, and entrechat is required for a ballet dancer to become fluent and articulate in his/her dance language (Hong, 2000). Without doing so, they cannot perform adequately. Taking this into account, literacy in one dance language does not necessarily equate to literacy in another.

Society's deep-rooted interest in dance has spurred the design of systems that capture and notate dance movements. Their use represents a very specific technology as they help reveal and record dance and body movement. One such example is Labanotation, a standardized linguistic system used for analyzing and archiving human motion. First published in 1928 by Rudolf Laban, Labanotation uses abstract symbols to define the direction of the movement, the part of the body doing the movement, the level of the movement, and the length of time it takes to do the movement. In this system, spatial distance, spatial relationships, transference of weight, center of weight, jumps, turns, body parts, paths, and floor plans can all be notated by specific symbols. These symbols are then transcribed onto a

A dance notation for the work *La Cachucha* by Friederich Albert Zorn. Courtesy of Wikimedia Commons.

scale (similar to that of a music staff) and provide dancers, choreographers, students, teachers, and researchers with smaller, kinetic units that can be easily understood and constructed (Laban, 1966).

Dance notation tools such as Labanotation are essential for those who wish to study and duplicate simple to complex movements while preserving the integrity of such movement. For academics, notation systems connect the kinesthetic aspect of dance to a visual and linguistic one, allowing for a more fluent construction of meaning. In other words, documenting movements through these notation systems is symbolically the same as writing words to be read.

But why is this important in the context of multiliteracies? What makes dance a form of literacy? Unlike other forms of expression, dance has a powerful capacity to reflect man's social, political, and cultural values creatively and aesthetically. Generations have each contributed, created, changed, and even perfected the art of dance to the extent that it is grounded as part of our tradition and communication. This form of representation provides for the creation of exceptional forms of meaning and understanding, as participants and observers use different cognitive and kinesthetic abilities than with more traditional literary practices.

As previously mentioned, a more encompassing and conceptual understanding of literacy allows us to accept dance as a literacy, where each dance element (rhythm, form, structure, style, tempo, theory, notation) is considered an important piece of that language. Rudolf Laban best sums this view of dance as a literacy in his explanation that movement is a type of language for people, and because of this it must be consciously mastered (Davies,

2005). In understanding dance in this context, we once again expand the meaning of literacy to be something much more complex than the traditional static text. In terms of dance notation, it also represents a type of literacy that is ultimately dependent on a dynamic and kinesthetic form.

29

Interpreting Body Language

The Original Literacy

Amanda P. Goodwin

Communicating through Body Language. Photograph by Amanda Goodwin.

Multiliteracies: Beyond Text and the Written Word, pages 131–135

How old is literacy? Did literacy predate the development of written language? Can literacy move beyond written symbols into using knowledge to gain meaning from visual clues such as body language? This chapter attempts to explore the larger construct of literacy and show how making meaning is as original to humans as movement and language.

Today, literacy is understood by most people as being limited to the ability to read and write text. Literate individuals are thought of as people who effectively decode, create, and gain meaning from written words leading to success in completing tasks or in understanding a larger set of ideas. Portraying this singular emphasis on written symbols, the first definition in the American Heritage Dictionary defines literate as "able to read or write" (literate, 2004). Yet it is the second definition, which defines literate as one who is "knowledgeable or educated in a particular field or fields" (literate, 2004) that allows us to truly look at the concept of literacy apart from text. By applying this association between literacy and knowledge, a case can be made that literacy, or being knowledgeable in gaining meaning from symbols or clues, existed long before the invention of writing systems.

Historically, "literacy" has existed in an alternative form that has depended on interpreting visual body cues rather than written symbols. Before written language, a literate individual effectively 'read' other people to obtain insight into situations. A person knowledgeable in body language could not only read the visual clues of others, but also present his or her own meanings in a clear manner. These effective nonverbal communication skills often meant the difference between prosperity and demise. Today, knowledge of body language, also known as nonverbal signals, continues to be a key to success.

Literacy in body language is different from knowledge of cultural gestures. Although it is difficult to completely separate these two concepts, the general consensus of researchers is that body language includes automatic responses to stimuli whereas gestures are taught through socialization. This debate goes back to Charles Darwin's 1872 text, *The Expression of the Emotions in Man and Animals*, in which Darwin argued that the majority of emotional expressions are determined from evolution. The field of nonverbal communication has swayed between automaticity and cultural interactions, but recent cross-cultural data show similarities in labeling expressions among more than 12 Western and non-Western cultures, including a remote preliterate culture in New Guinea. In studies by Izard (1971), Ekman and Friesen (1970), and Ekman, Sorensn, and Friesen (1969), people of various cultures were presented with pictures of people from different cultures portraying assorted emotions. These researchers found that Westerners and non-West-

Plate #2 showing subjects with different emotions from Charles Darwin, *The Expression of the Emotions in Man and Animals*. London: John Murray, 1872. First edition, second issue, p. 180.

erners alike were able to label the emotions of people from other cultures (Segerstrale & Molnar, 1997). The ability to read facial expressions across cultures emphasizes the universality of many body language examples and the importance of literacy in reading nonverbal signals.

Many examples of body language signals are common because they are automatic reactions to situations that stem from our human survival instincts. For example, the reaction of fleeing from danger or taking an intimidating stance when facing an enemy helps protect us from attack. Other nonverbal clues provide insight into feelings and motivate actions. "Facial expressions motivate us to act and allow us to influence others. Our ability to decode facial expressions determines the behaviors we choose in response to others (avoiding an angry person, helping a depressed person, etc.)" (Remland, 2000). The automaticity of such reactions, for example,

"We are bored." Photograph by Miriam Lipsky.

blushing from embarrassment, startling as a result of surprise, and smiling due to joy often occur automatically and provide authentic clues to feelings. Although people can try to mimic these responses, most phony cues are easily discerned, and therefore, individuals who are literate in reading body language can use these nonverbal signals to determine the truthfulness and underlying feelings of a respondent (Remland, 2000). For example, in a meta-analysis of 45 studies asking participants to answer questions falsely, certain nonverbal cues showed up in a significant number of trials. These visual clues included pupil dilation, less blinking, less gazing, and fewer movements of the head and body (Zuckerman & Driver, 1985). Understanding these nonverbal cues can help literate individuals gain insight into the veracity of statements and behaviors.

As a literacy, body language has characteristics similar to written language. Like traditional literacy, which requires written symbols to communicate meaning, body language is communicated through several channels including facial expression, eye contact, gesture, posture, and appearance. Also similar to language is the storage of nonverbal signals into a lexicon, although while there is no universal written or spoken lexicon, because of the automaticity and cross-cultural interpretations of many body language cues, the lexicon for body language is somewhat universal across cultures (Remland, 2000, p. 23). In addition, instances of body language can be classified by purpose just like texts can be classified by genre. Such purposes include expressing emotion, communicating interpersonal attitudes, accompanying and supporting speech, self-preservation, and use in rituals (Remland, 2000).

Literacy in body language includes different levels of effectiveness at interpreting and communicating. Large individual differences in terms of sending (encoding), receiving (decoding), and regulation (management) of nonverbal communication contribute to the highly popular concept of emotional intelligence (Manusov & Patterson, 2006). For example, researchers have found that the few people who are able to detect deception beyond chance are particularly effective at noticing inconsistencies in nonverbal cues and have a strong motivation to observe and analyze human behavior (O'Sullivan, 2005). Interpreting, expressing, and controlling nonverbal messages are critical to social, professional, and ultimately financial success.

The constructs of literacy and reading body language overlap in their purpose—to decode, create, and interpret meaning. It is this overlap that makes knowledge of body language an important alternative literacy in both history and modern society. In fact, the universality of body language cues shows that literacy of nonverbal communication crosses cultural, geographic, and social class boundaries. Individual differences in the skills of people to interpret body language have significant consequences for success. This is where education and schools must step in and help teach students how to be literate in reading body language cues. With the great emphasis on academic standards and the No Child Left Behind legislation, instruction in life skills such as effective nonverbal communication has largely disappeared from the curriculum. Literacy in body language has been an important component for success throughout history. As educators, we must insist students become literate in reading body language so that they can successfully negotiate the vital channels of nonverbal communication, detecting deceptions and accurately conveying meanings that lead to both personal and professional success.

30

Baseball Signs

Visual Literacy at Play

Miriam Lipsky

A coach at a college baseball game signaling his players. Photograph by Miriam Lipsky.

Multiliteracies: Beyond Text and the Written Word, pages 137–140

Children attending school often bring with them unique literacies related to their experiences outside of school. These experiences may come from their families, their early schooling (preschool or daycare), or arts, sports, and other activities in which they participate. For children who participate in T-ball or baseball, they may bring to school literacy in the signs and signals of baseball—a creative type of sign language with a "vocabulary" understood only by members of the same team.

Unlike many types of literacies, where the goal is to communicate a message that can be understood by many people, with baseball signs, the goal is for the message to be understood only by a few select people: those who are members of a specific sports team. This sign language is used to communicate from catcher to pitcher, infielder to outfielder, manager to base coach, base coach to base runners, and various other combinations of team members. By using this "secret" visual language, coaches (usually the third base coach) are able to communicate with their players about what they want them to do, from trying to steal a base to hitting a particular pitch in a certain way. For example, the job of the third base coach is to give signals to the batter and the base runners. All of these players must be sure to look at the third base coach so that they know what to do once a pitch is thrown. The team may have many signals for different plays, but there is a "key" or "indicator" signal, and all signals given before this key signal are invalid. Usually, the sign directly following the key signal indicates the play to be made. For example, according to the Baseball Canada web site (http://www.baseball.ca/), the following list shows some possible signals which may exist in a team's system:

1. Key or indicator = Touching the face with the right hand
2. Sacrifice/Bunt = Right hand to baseball cap
3. Steal = Right hand to ear
4. Take a pitch = Right hand to left arm
5. Hit and Run = Right hand to chest
6. Swing Away = Left hand to right arm (batter's discretion)

In a game, the third base coach may give the following signal sequence before a pitch is thrown: right hand to ear/left hand to right arm/right hand to chest/touch face with right hand/right hand to ear/right hand to baseball cap.

If you were a player on the field, what would you do, based on this sequence of signals? If you would steal a base, you are correct! Note that the signal for stealing a base was the first signal given after the "key," which was touching the face with the right hand. If you were the batter, what would you do in this signal sequence? If you would sacrifice or bunt, then you would be correct, since the signal to sacrifice or bunt was the second signal given after the key signal.

The signs of baseball are so important in the game that various stories exist in baseball lore regarding the lengths that coaches and managers would go to in order to communicate with their teams. For example, according to Stone (2003), one coach who was ejected from a minor league game returned dressed in the mascot's uniform to continue sending signals to his team. Another coach who was ejected from a minor league game climbed a light pole outside the ballpark and sent in signals to his players and assistants from there.

In an average nine-inning baseball game, it has been estimated that approximately 1,000 silent signals are given (Stone, 2003). With signs being so important to communication in baseball, it seems that opposing teams would have a vested interest in learning the sign language of their opponents, and indeed they do. In order to deal with this problem, some

Signaling a player on base. Photograph by Miriam Lipsky.

teams change their signals for each game; other teams have been known to change their signals every three innings, and still other teams have individual signals for each player (Stone, 2003). When the catcher is relaying signals to the pitcher about what pitch to throw, he will shield his signal hand between his knee and his baseball glove to ensure that the first and third base coaches cannot see the signal he is sending. Of course, with all these complicated signals, there are potential errors. The Red Sox in the 1970s had signals that required players to add and subtract various numbers of touches given by the coach in order to figure out the play to be made. Stone (2003) relays a story about outfielder Bernie Carbo, who was caught and tagged out while stealing a base one night.

His manager Darrell Johnson angrily confronted him, asking Carbo what he had seen to make him run. "Two plus two," Carbo replied. "That's four—the take sign," said Johnson. "The steal is five." "Damn!" said Carbo. "I added wrong."

To those who have not played the game, the gyrations, touches, and other signals that make up baseball sign language may seem almost comical at times, but to the players, this unique literacy is a critical part of playing the game. Unlike other literacies that seek to convey a message to all viewers, this secretive literacy is only understood by the members of a particular team. Children who participate in baseball as an extracurricular sport may bring this literacy in the secret sign language of baseball to school with them. Whether this will help these children acquire the more traditional literacies taught in school is certainly debatable, but understanding their team's baseball signs may broaden students' concepts of communication in general and other alternative literacies in particular, and represents a particularly interesting type of multiliteracy.

31

Order of Magnitude Literacy

Sheree T. Sharpe

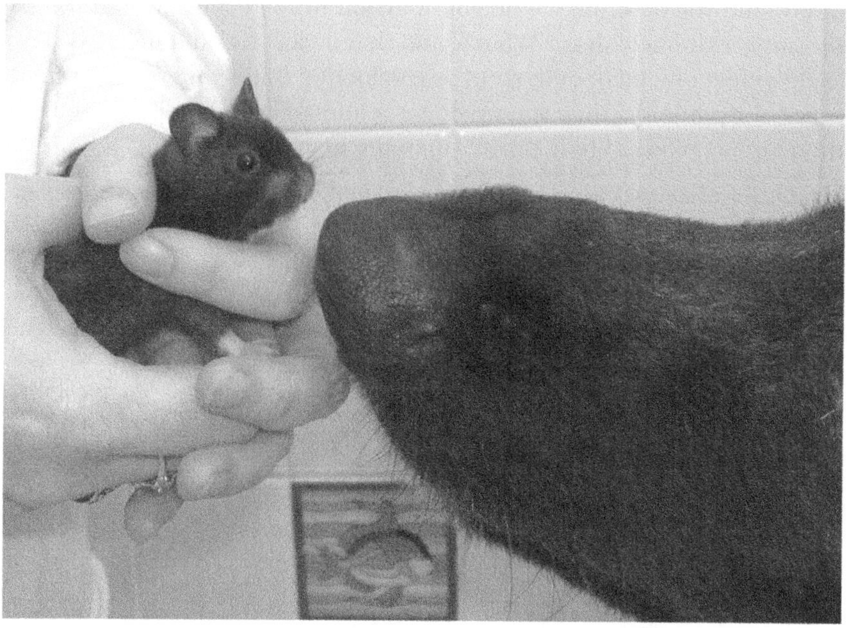

"Noses large and small." Photograph by Megan Lipsky.

Multiliteracies: Beyond Text and the Written Word, pages 141–143

The Oxford English Dictionary states that order of magnitude is "a class in a system of classification determined by size, typically in powers of ten." One number that differs from a second number by one order of magnitude is ten times bigger than the second number. For example, the mass of the Earth is one order of magnitude greater than that of Mars—in other words it has ten times as much mass. The number 7 is three orders of magnitude less than 7,000 because 7 times 10 to the third power (7×10^3) is equal to 7,000.

Order of magnitude is an important literacy because it allows us to classify very large magnitudes and very small magnitudes by comparing them to other objects. It is widely understood and used in the scientific community but not widely understood or used by the general public. For example, how would you describe the height of an ant to somebody? Would you say the ant is extremely short? What would that mean? It could mean as short as three feet one inch, or as short as two inches. But if you were literate in order of magnitude, then you would say a human being's height is roughly three orders of magnitude greater than the height of an ant.

Order of magnitude is usually used to make very approximate comparisons. Order of magnitude can be used to describe the difference between size of numbers, area, currency, frequency, length, mass, speed, temperature, time, volume, and more. The difficulty increases as we are required to express and employ numbers as large as the radius of the universe and as small as the diameter of a proton. These can be described using prefixes in the International system of units, for example Yotta (10^{24}), Giga (10^9), Kilometers (10^3), Micrometers (10^{-6}), Nanometers (10^{-9}), and Atto (10^{-18}).

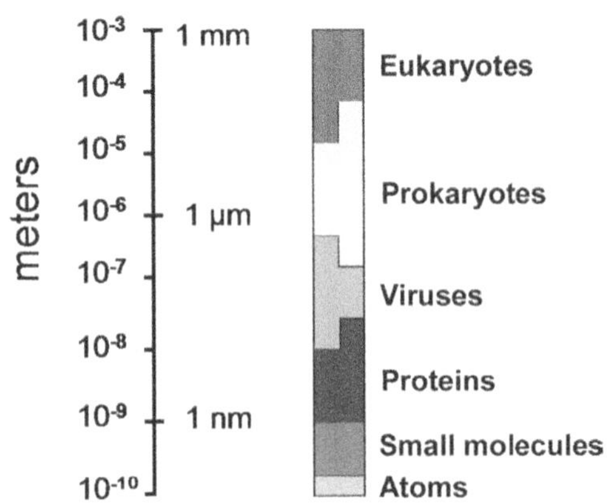

"Relative scales of eukaryotes, prokaryotes, viruses, proteins and atoms" Courtesy of Wikimedia Commons.

If someone asked you how far the earth is from the sun (about 10^{11} meters), or how many cells are in the human body (over 10^{14}), what would you say? Would you say "a lot"? If you were literate in order of magnitude, then you may say something like: the earth is eleven orders of magnitude from the sun, after explaining what an order of magnitude is. This answer will give the person a much more specific idea of how large something is, rather than just saying, "It's large."

When comparing magnitudes it is often helpful to use an order of magnitude scale. In order to do this one must be literate in order of magnitude. For example, literacy in order of magnitude can make the process of comparing the loudness of a sound or the brightness of a star much easier.

Order of magnitude can be used to describe the size of something as small as bacteria. For example, according to the diagram above, atoms are approximately seven orders of magnitudes smaller than eukaryotes. Being able to describe the size of bacteria is very significant to scientists. For scientists to accurately perform experiments to find cures, they need to be able to have a precise comparison of very small scales of bacteria.

Order of magnitude is also used by the Richter scale. Charles Richter published a paper about the Richter scale in 1935. Richter created this scale to measure the magnitude of earthquakes in Southern California as early as 1932. The Richter magnitude scale assigns a single number to quantify the amount of seismic energy released by an earthquake (Hough, 2007). Literacy in order of magnitude allows understanding of how the Richter scale calculates the magnitude of an earthquake.

The true usefulness of order of magnitude comes in to play when scientists say that an earthquake was micro, moderate, or great. It's the magnitude of the earthquake in orders of magnitude. Micro earthquakes occur all the time around the world in places like California and Alaska in the United States; they occur about 8,000 times per day, and they are not felt. Moderate earthquakes occur 800 times per year and may or may not be destructive. Great earthquakes occur less frequently, about once every 20 years, but they are devastating. Having an understanding of an earthquake's magnitude can save your life. But literacy in order of magnitude can also give you a deeper understanding of the intensity of the earthquake's magnitude. Literacy in order of magnitudes is, in fact, related to education because students need to be prepared for their roles as future scientists.

32

Becoming Literate in the Language of Dogs

A Literacy That Could Save Your Life

Miriam Lipsky

"Best Friends." Photograph by Miriam Lipsky.

Multiliteracies: Beyond Text and the Written Word, pages 145–151

Reading signs can keep individuals safe in their environment. Signs such as "danger," "keep out," "high voltage," "wrong way—do not enter," and "poison" exist as environmental print both in words and symbols in most communities in the developed world. Similarly, being able to read the body language of domesticated animals, specifically dogs, can keep people safe in their environments. Yet despite the obvious importance of this area, literacy involving the body language of domesticated animals is rarely discussed.

According to the Centers for Disease Control and Prevention (CDC), each year in the United States more than 4.7 million people are bitten by "man's best friend" (CDC, 2008). Approximately 800,000 of those people will seek medical attention for their dog bites, with about half of those bitten being children. Of those who are injured, almost half, or 386,000 require treatment in an emergency room. Unfortunately, about a dozen people die each year from injuries caused by dog bites. Although most dogs are truly wonderful pets, some are very territorial or unfriendly to strangers, and some strays, especially those running in packs, can pose a danger to people.

People in certain professions, such as postal workers and meter readers, are at particular risk of injury from dog bites due to the nature of their daily work. There is even an annual National Dog Bite Prevention Week (the third full week of May). Of the dog bite-related injuries occurring in the United States, children from ages five to nine have the highest incidence of injury, but people of all ages can be affected.

Clearly, people should have an interest in becoming literate in the body language of dogs in order to keep them safe. For dog lovers, of course, un-

This dog's facial expressions convey that he is alert. Photograph by Miriam Lipsky.

derstanding the body language of their pets is an added benefit, since most dogs are quite friendly (unless threatened) and communicate many things other than aggression!

Because dogs do not have the ability to speak (aside from barking, whining, and certain other vocalizations), they communicate mostly with their bodies and body parts, much like their ancestors, wolves, have always done. Aside from overall body posture, the parts of a dog that are mainly used for communication are the tail, eyes, ears, and mouth.

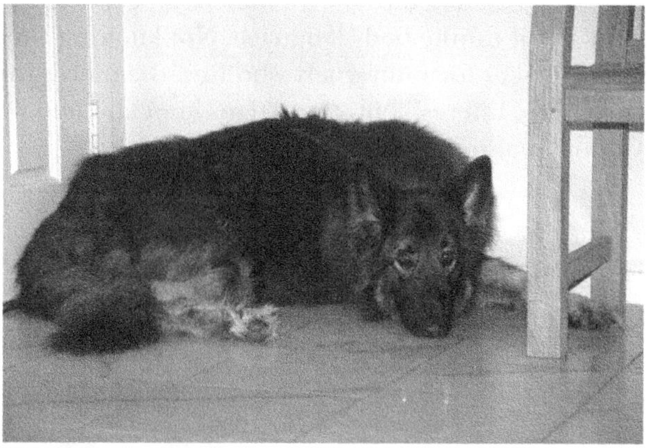

This dog's facial expressions and body posture convey that he is relaxed. Photo by Miriam Lipsky.

This dog's facial expressions convey that he is alert and on guard. Photograph by Miriam Lipsky.

These communication tools make it easy for dogs to communicate with, and be understood by, other dogs. Understanding the subtleties of the positioning of the dogs' body, tail, eyes, ears, and mouth can help a person to distinguish between a friendly dog and an aggressive one, between a playful situation and a potentially life-threatening one.

The drawings below illustrate some of the most common messages that dogs convey with their facial expressions and body postures (illustrations used with the permission of Bash Dibra). They can indicate confidence, aggression, submission, and other emotional states. These are the key types of canine body language that must be identified, if people are to be literate in the basic aspects of canine body language. Not knowing these signs can have dire consequences for individuals who find themselves frequently in the presence of dogs. Interestingly, these signs are exhibited by dogs of all sizes, from Chihuahuas to St. Bernards.

These dogs are both alert. Their ears are pricked up and eyes are wide open. The dog on the left has his mouth closed for sniffing; the one on the right has his mouth relaxed and open, and may be panting.

This dog's facial expression conveys the fact that he is relaxed. Notice that it is similar to the alert expression, except that the ears are halfway back and slightly outward.

The dog in this illustration is showing submission, with his ears back, mouth pulled back, and eyes averted.

These two dogs are showing anxiety. The key facial features are the narrowed eyes, ears partially back, and mouths that are closed and tense.

An anxious dog can quickly become a fearful dog, as his perception of the situation changes, leading to possible aggression, as shown in the next set of illustrations.

At first glance the aggressive dogs may look quite similar, but there are some key differences, most notably in the ears. The dominant dog has his

All three of these dogs are showing aggression, but of different sorts. The dog on the left is displaying dominant aggression, the one in the center shows fear aggression, and the one on the right shows guarding aggression.

Three body postures: dominant, submissive, and relaxed. The dog in the center is a dominant dog, standing tall and proud with his head and tail held high, ears pricked, and fur fluffed up. The dog on the left is showing submission, with his tail tucked between his legs and ears back. The dog on the right, with his head up and tail straight out is showing a typical stance of a confident, relaxed dog.

ears pricked up, the guarding dog has his ears turned outward to be able to listen for sounds of danger and the ears are pulled in closer to his head in case he needs to fight, and the dog displaying fear aggression has his ears laid back. For humans interpreting these expressions, the key difference is that the dog with its ears laid back will be more likely to back off if the perceived threat goes away. The dominant and guarding dogs are more likely to bite.

For children, the CDC offers these tips for teaching children basic safety around dogs and preventing dog bites:

- Do not approach an unfamiliar dog.
- Do not run from a dog and scream.
- Remain motionless (e.g., "be still like a tree") when approached by an unfamiliar dog.
- If knocked over by a dog, roll into a ball and lie still (e.g., "be still like a log").
- Do not play with a dog unless supervised by an adult.
- Immediately report stray dogs or dogs displaying unusual behavior to an adult.
- Avoid direct eye contact with a dog.
- Do not disturb a dog that is sleeping, eating, or caring for puppies.
- Do not pet a dog without allowing it to see and sniff you first.
- If bitten, immediately report the bite to an adult. (CDC, 2008)

An understanding of animal body language, as in the case of dogs, suggests a type of physical and tactical literacy than extends itself to other areas as well. Human body language can be very important for children (and adults) to understand. Howard Gardner, who is the author of a large body of work on individual competence in the framework of multiple intelligences, discusses interpersonal intelligence, which is concerned with understanding the intentions, desires, and motivations of others (Gardner, 1993). Those people who are successful at interpreting the body language of dogs (or other animals) may possess a unique form of Gardner's "interpersonal" intelligence—something more like "inter*species*" intelligence. This type of intelligence can be valuable in accurately interpreting the messages which others may try to convey; messages which are often non-verbal. The work of Erving Goffman (1988) shows us how the advertising industry uses information on the body language of primates (including human beings) to depict certain gender roles and other messages in visual images. Awareness that body language conveys a message that may or may not be in accordance with a person's verbal message can help people to accurately decipher communication from others. Interestingly, the lack of this skill at "reading" the body language (including facial expressions) of others is one of the hallmarks of Autistic Spectrum Disorders, specifically Asperger's Syndrome, and one of the problems faced by autistic children. The inability to correctly interpret nonverbal communication makes it difficult, if not impossible, for autistic children to understand the subtle, or even not-so-subtle, messages that others try to convey through nonverbal means such as body posture, facial expression, and gestures.

Many children love animals. Providing them with information or training on how to interpret the body language of their canine family members, as well as unfamiliar dogs they may encounter, may help them to sharpen their "interpersonal" type of intelligence, as well as keeping them safe. This type of intelligence can help them to more accurately interpret the messages (verbal and nonverbal) that others try to convey. As an added benefit, the more people can become educated in the literacy of the body language of man's best friend, the greater the chances that we can reduce the number of injuries resulting from dog bites each year. After all, dogs do not know that we humans do not understand "dog language," so they communicate with us in the way they would with members of their own species. It is through our unfortunate lack of fluency in this language that some misunderstandings occur, and a dog may feel the need to bite, because his warnings and other communications have not been understood. Similarly, if people can become more sensitive to the nonverbal signals of their fellow human beings, perhaps there will be fewer misunderstandings or reasons for humans to "bite back" at others, either verbally or otherwise.

33

Etiquette

The Literacy of Success

Amanda P. Goodwin

"Princess tea party." Photograph by Amanda Goodwin.

Multiliteracies: Beyond Text and the Written Word, pages 153–157

In modern society, etiquette is an example of a multiliteracy that has true social, political, and economic effects. Although the concept may seem old-fashioned, today's etiquette rules encompass both traditional norms such as politely accompanying a request with the word "please" to updated versions that include cell phone and internet etiquette. Like most multiliteracies, the concept of etiquette, or "the practices and forms prescribed by social convention or by authority" (Etiquette, 2006) differs from culture to culture and from situation to situation. Because of these constant modifications, successful persons must be literate in interpreting and mimicking the etiquette of various environments. Manners make a difference. We must know, learn, and fine-tune our understanding as etiquette retains tradition and adapts to technology and globalization.

There are many examples of how business people must adapt their etiquette based on surroundings. For example, business meetings in the United States use a firm handshake as part of meeting or making deals, whereas in Japan the handshake is replaced with the more traditional bow when meeting, getting attention, showing gratitude, or expressing sympathy (Kwintessential, n.d).

Etiquette also differs by setting. Etiquette for teachers in elementary school environments differs from the etiquette of professors in a university setting. This can be seen in the dress, language, and classroom setup. This chapter will explore how mom's timeless etiquette concepts merge with modern technologies, arguing that etiquette is a necessary literacy in the business world and beyond.

Etiquette is essential when applying for a job. Similar to any literacy, etiquette has codes that must be learned and followed. For example, resumes must be accompanied by a cover letter describing your interest in the position and qualifications. Cover letters should be tailored to the position, including information from your resume that is pertinent to the job in question. Resumes must also follow specific formatting guidelines (Toppel Career Center, 2007).

While some rules of business etiquette are well publicized, other more hidden rules can help applicants stand out. In a survey of 150 business executives, almost nine out of ten administrators report that writing a thank-you note after a job interview improves the odds of getting the job, yet only 49% of candidates interviewed actually sent a thank you note. "It's a differentiator," says Anna Post, a business etiquette trainer with the Emily Post Institute. "Say you're applying for a job and you have gone through the interview process. You write a thank-you note to the person who interviewed you, and your competitor doesn't. All other things being equal, it could make quite a big difference" (quoted in Cho, 2007). Experts even suggest writing the thank you note within 24 hours (Langford, 2005). Similarly, looking the interviewer in the eye and greeting the person with both first and last name are important aspects of etiquette that make a good first impression (Sabath, 2002). In fact, books on business etiquette go so far as to describe in detail how to shake hands in a business environment:

> Clasp the other person's palm with your palm, rather than fingers to fingers. Your grip should be firm. Hold someone's hand too loosely and it's possible you will earn the dreaded description of being 'a dead fish.' Do not, however, be so firm that you squeeze the other person's hand too hard. Rather than causing pain of any sort, simply apply a little pressure. (Sabath, 2002)

Literacy in business etiquette transfers beyond the job application process to the actual job setting. According to American etiquette expert, Letitia Baldrige

> Good manners are cost-effective. They increase the quality of life in the workplace, contribute to optimum employee morale, embellish the company image, and hence play a major role in generating profit. On the other hand, negative behavior, whether based on selfishness, carelessness, or ignorance, can cost a person a promotion, even a job. (Baldrige, 1990)

A lack of knowledge and use of etiquette can result in loss of revenue and clients. In a study by the U.S. Office of Consumer Affairs, the importance of etiquette was highlighted with data showing that as many as 91% of unhappy customers do not do business with a company that has offended the customer. Another finding showed the effect of poor etiquette on reputation, reporting that the average unhappy customer will share the story with at least nine other people, and 13% of unhappy customers will share the story with more than twenty people (DuPont, 1998).

Within the workplace, experts cite both abstract and more concrete rules of etiquette. For example, respect, dedication, and professionalism are all important abstract aspects of creating a positive business culture, yet what do these concepts look like in terms of specific business settings? This is where more specific rules of etiquette must be learned and acquired within your business setting. For example, DuPont (1998) suggests that you should dress for the position you want, not the position you have. To do that, one must be familiar with etiquette rules for dressing, yet flexible enough to adapt these rules to observations of the realities of how superiors are dressing in the workplace.

With the increase in technology, the ability to adapt timeless rules of etiquette to modern society is increasingly important. In Emily Post's 1922 seminal work on etiquette, *Etiquette in Society, in Business, in Politics and at Home*, Post includes an entire section of business etiquette on smoking in front of a "lady" (Post, 1922). Today, with smoking prohibited in most business locations, business people must adapt the timeless concept of respect for others when smoking to modern settings. Similarly, Post's major work includes no rules for etiquette involving email, text messaging, cell phone usage, internet protocol, communication on websites such as facebook.com or myspace.com, or even on internet dating because such things did not exist in her time. The ability to transfer old-fashioned concepts of etiquette to modern technology is vital to both business and personal success.

Such transfer has resulted in concrete etiquette rules for modern technologies. For example, Lipscomb and colleagues (2007) studied the cell phone usage of 383 young adults in a geographically diverse area and found significant agreement among users on appropriate and inappropriate uses of cell phones. According to this study,

> Respondents considered inappropriate situations for cell phone usage to include during worship/church, during class, in a library and in a movie theatre during a movie. Respondents considered it to be appropriate to use cell phones while on public transportation, in a supermarket, and to use a hands-free set while driving. (Lipscomb, 2007)

With that said, flexibility continues to be important because the study found specific differences as a function of geographic regions, gender, and employment status.

Internet communication etiquette, termed "netiquette," has also developed formal rules. "Netiquette, or network etiquette, is the contemporary term for the proper way we communicate and interact with each other using email over the Internet" (Yale University Library, 2007). Yale University staff development suggests following these rules for netiquette: Use a strong subject line, include the most important ideas in the first part of the email, keep paragraphs short, proofread before sending, use spell check and grammar check, do not share confidential information, do not share your password, do not forward chain letters, keep acronyms to a minimum, do not forward an email without the authors knowledge and consent, and so on.

Etiquette is a multiliteracy that is both timeless and constantly evolving to include changes in society and advances in technology. Knowledge of etiquette yields power, as shown by better job opportunities, an improved reputation, more respect for one's ideas, and improved overall support. Individuals must be literate in rules of etiquette, and must also apply, observe, and adapt those rules to various settings. Although there are no courses on etiquette in our classrooms, the socialization work of schools, along with family lessons on manners, provides a base of rules that adapt over time and among settings. In fact, knowledge of etiquette customs contributes to success as much as any part of one's resume. Even in life, "The ability to handle yourself properly . . . outweighs even your technical skills" (DuPont, 1998).

34

Ebonics as a Literacy

Sheree T. Sharpe

Phrases
Phat = good
Fly = good
Supafly = very good
Shortiez = children or younger people
Papers = money
Grill = gold teeth
Yo = Hello
Sup? = How are you?
Dope/Dizzle = good
Whack = bad
Peeps = people
Nizzle = friend
Dawg = friend
5-0 = Police

Phrases in Black Dialect or Ebonics.

Ebonics was created in 1973 by a group of black scholars who disliked the negative connotations of terms like "Nonstandard Negro English." Ebonics is a blend of the words ebony, meaning "black," and phonics, meaning "the study of sound." The term *Ebonics* is thought of as black speech (Rickford, 2003). But this is not true. Not all African Americans speak Ebon-

Multiliteracies: Beyond Text and the Written Word, pages 159–161

ics, and there are non-African Americans who speak Ebonics because they grew up in the communities where it is spoken (Rubba, 1997).

Since 1996, some have considered Ebonics an alternative term for African American Vernacular English (AAVE), but others consider it an antonym of Black English, therefore a language other than English and thus rejecting AAVE. Ebonics has associations with dialects spoken elsewhere in the Black Diaspora, such as Jamaica or Nigeria (Rickford, 2003). There are two theories about the origins of this form of speech: a "dialectal hypothesis" and a "Creole hypothesis." The "dialectal hypothesis" asserts that Ebonics is a dialect of English. The "Creole hypothesis" asserts that Ebonics evolved out of a pidgin language that developed in West Africa as a result of the slave trade and commercial trade between Africans and Europeans during the 16th–19th centuries (Rubba, 1997).

In today's society, literacy in only reading and writing is not adequate; we also need to be literate at different languages. In Miami, for example, knowledge of Spanish is almost essential in order to communicate with a large part of the population. What about literacy in Ebonics? What about having the ability to communicate with people who speak Ebonics? Across the United States there are black communities where Ebonics is spoken. Ebonics not only shows up in communities, but also in written literature and rap music. The children of these communities are entering schools speaking Ebonics. If we want to teach these children standard or academic English, then we must be literate in Ebonics.

In December 1996, the term Ebonics became widely known in the United States when the Oakland (California) School Board recognized Ebonics as the "primary" language of its majority African American students and resolved to take Ebonics into account when teaching them Standard English (Ramirez et al, 2005; Rickford, 2003). This should not be our only goal. We should also teach Ebonics in our schools as another form of speech.

Don't be trippin'	=	Do not be anxious, don't worry
Keepin' it real	=	Keep things in perspective
Livin' it large	=	Living a prosperous life
To smoke	=	To shoot
To bust a cap	=	To shoot
Check yo' self	=	Watch what you say or do
You all up in my grill	=	You're in my face
Off da hook	=	very good

Phrases in Black Dialect or Ebonics.

Nobel Prize winning journalist Toni Morrison remarked (in an interview in *The New Republic* on March 21, 1981) that:

> [T]he language, only the language.... It is the thing that black people love so much—the saying of words, holding them on the tongue, experimenting with them, playing with them. It's a love, a passion. Its function is like a preacher's: to make you stand up out of your seat, make you lose yourself and hear yourself. The worst of all possible things that could happen would be to lose that language. There are certain things I cannot say without recourse to my language. It's terrible to think that a child with five different present tenses comes to school to be faced with books that are less than his own language. And then to be told things about his language, which is him, that are sometimes permanently damaging. He may never know the etymology of Africanisms in his language, not even know that "hip" is a real word or that "the dozens" meant something. This is a really cruel fallout of racism. I know the standard English. I want to use it to help restore the other language, the lingua franca. (Rickford & Rickford, 2000)

African Americans continue to speak Ebonics for self-preservation. Ebonics ties them to family, community, their peers, and African American history (Thompson, 2004). Should we ask them to replace Ebonics with standard English? Or should we ask them to also learn standard English? When a teacher tells an African American to speak only standard English in the classroom, then the teacher is taking away that student's ability to be involved in the classroom discourse, if that student has to censor the only way they know how to communicate.

Ebonics is equated with ignorance, backwardness, and a lower socioeconomic status, instead of a crucial tie that connects speakers to the African American community, particularly urban and rural communities (Thompson, 2004). African American students should be allowed to use their speech of origin to learn the standard English. Ebonics should not only be a literacy in the communities that speak Ebonics, but also a literacy for everyone who comes in contact with Ebonics speakers.

African Americans who speak Ebonics are treated as inferior because they are not able to communicate with others in standard English. But African Americans who speak standard English are considered "not black" if they don't speak Ebonics (Thompson, 2004). It is important for us to be Ebonics literate in order to respect the many cultures that make us American.

35

Visual Representation of Mathematics

Gabriel Quintana

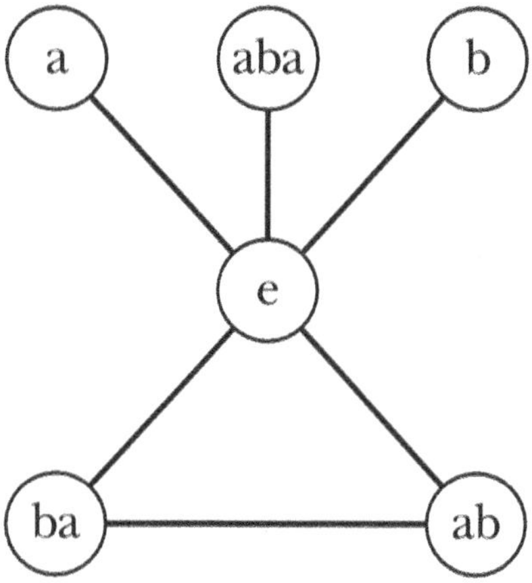

Cycle Diagram Representing Organizational Structure in Group Theory. English Wikipedia 2006, March 10, 2006.

Many technical and academic fields have a language system that is unique to them. These language systems allow for the comprehension, progression, and further analysis of subjects within a field. One such example is seen with the emergence of the visual representation of mathematics. With the help of new technologies, these visual representations enhance the mathematical edification of its users and further proliferates the advance of the discipline. The subject of mathematics

Multiliteracies: Beyond Text and the Written Word, pages 163–166

is separated into many distinctive fields, each of which has been influenced by the recent developments in visualizations. In this chapter, I present some of the mathematical fields influenced by visualization processes and technologies, and develop its relationship to the overarching classification of alternative literacies.

The first field of mathematics discussed in this essay for the purposes of describing visual representations in mathematics is that of structure, which includes the subjects of number theory, abstract algebra, group theory, and order theory (Eves, 1990). All of these subjects require stability and structure through the use of rigorous definitions and axioms, necessitating the need for organization through visual representations (Rusin, 2000).

The next field of mathematics with visual ramifications in the formation of alternative literacies is the area of space. Space includes Euclidean geometry, trigonometry, topology, and fractal geometry (Eves, 1990). The use of visualization during the past twenty years has been essential for the development of mathematical space. For instance, fractal geometry and, to a similar extent, modern topology arose out of the development of computer software in the 1970s; without the visualization processes of such software, these fields would not exist today (Abraham, 2002).

Another field in mathematics affected by the overarching theme of visual literacies is the mathematics of change, which includes the topics of calculus, differential equations, and chaos theory (Eves, 1990). In calculus, many prob-

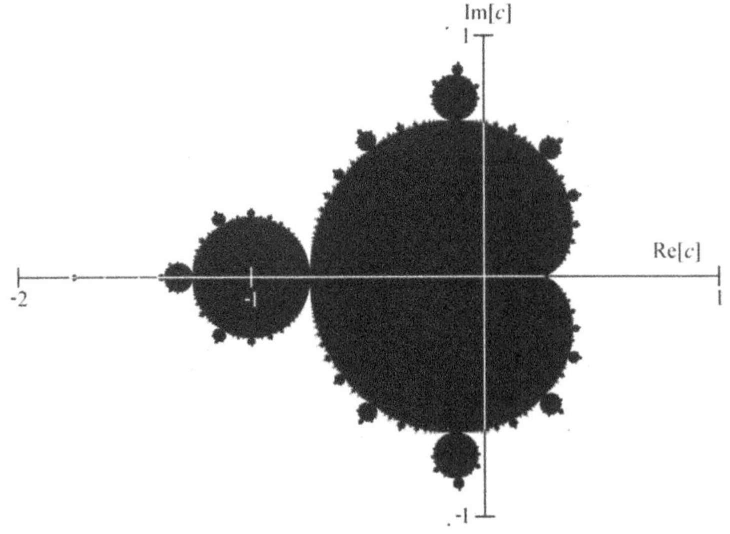

The Mandelbrot Set, a Component of Fractal Geometry. English Wikipedia 2005, October 8, 2005.

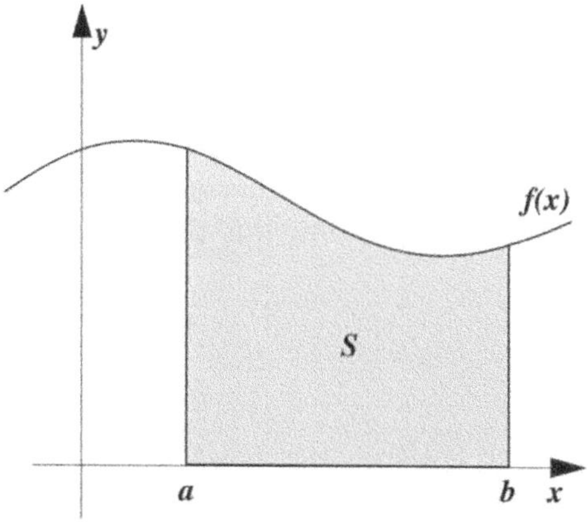

The Integral as Area Under the Curve. English Wikipedia 2006, October 08, 2006.

lems require finding some area, *S*, under the curve for some function $f(x)$ between two points (a, b). Textually, it requires mathematical understanding in interpreting some type of special symbology. Graphically, however, it is easier to understand the meaning of an integral of a function.

Another area of interest in benefit of the development of visualizations is the field of discrete mathematics, which includes topics such as combinatorics, cryptography, and graph theory (Eves, 1990). For instance, in cryptography, extensive, redundant security codes meant to protect online passwords are simplified through the use of visualizations such as matrices. Without these visualizations, it would be very difficult and inefficient to interpret encrypted codes. Yet deciphering these codes still requires a substantial amount of visual literacy, especially as the complexity in creating these codes increases.

The last area of interest in the visualization of mathematics is the field of applied mathematics, which includes mathematical physics and statistics. The use of statistics permeates many of the social sciences, and hence its practical implications are substantially important for the overall well-being of social structures. Therefore, critically understanding the results of statistical analysis through the use of visualizations has allowed social scientists to more accurately describe phenomena and offer better solutions to problems than ever before.

So what do these descriptions tell us about the nature of the literacies found in the visual representation of mathematics? For one, the outlined areas of mathematics constitute many different ways of knowing, learning, and communicating about mathematics. Second is their range of complexities. For instance, many of the visualizations of mathematical concepts allow the novice to envision the argument, while permitting the professional to investigate the mathematical phenomenon at a more complex level. In this context, an important characteristic of multiliteracies can be seen—that is, they allow for a more approachable understanding of traditional concepts while letting once abstract ideas come into the concrete world.

36

Medical Symbols, Shorthand, and Signage

Maribel G. Harder

Caduceus symbol. Drawing by Rama. Vectorized with Inkscape by Eliot Lash. March 26, 2006. Courtesy of Rama and Eliot Lash.

Society's symbols truly do reflect its values (Lahey, 1999). Nowhere is this more evident than in the field of medicine. Symbols such as the white coat serve many purposes: communicating hope, honor, and professional distance. In recent times, receiving this symbol in a White Coat

Multiliteracies: Beyond Text and the Written Word, pages 167–170

Ceremony has become a rite of passage (Jones, 1999). Among the more well-known symbols of medicine is the single serpent-entwined staff of Asklepios. This symbol carries a fascinating history that provides significant insight into our culturally based views of medicine.

As Lankshear has stated, literacy is best understood "as a sociocultural practice...in the context of social, cultural, political, economic, historical practices" of which it is a part (Lankshear, 1999, p. 13). Within this position, the single-serpented staff of Aesculapius, the Greek god of healing, carries insightful meaning. In his essay entitled "Serpents, Staffs, and the Emblems of Medicine," Nathan Williams notes that for many centuries and throughout various cultures, serpents have been associated with both healing and death, being both worshipped and feared. This dualistic nature symbolizes "the struggle between life and death as well as the potential for resurrection and immortality" (Williams, 1999, p. 475). In addition, the serpent has been associated with the role of messenger between this world and the underworld, thus signifying both the aspirations and perils associated with medical practice. When pursued with wisdom and benevolence, medicine is often capable of great healing. However, illness and death can still occur.

This dualism is evident in the Old Testament book of Numbers, where venomous snakes are biting and killing many Israelites. In this text, the Lord sends Moses to create a bronze snake on a pole so that when anyone is bitten by a snake and looks at the bronze snake, he survives (Numbers 21:4–9). The connection between serpent and staff is also evident in the book of Exodus, where the Lord commands Moses and Aaron to throw their staff before the Pharaoh, where it becomes a snake as a sign of their being sent from God. The staff itself also plays a pivotal role in Moses' journey with the Israelites. He is commanded to raise it before the parting of the Red Sea (Exodus 14:16–18), to strike it against a rock to provide water for the thirsty Israelites (Exodus 17:1–7), and to hold it up in the air to ensure victory over the Amalekites (Exodus 17:8–15). This "staff of God" thus represents a connection to a higher, supernatural power and chosen leadership.

In fact, "the brass serpent of Moses was a very popular Renaissance motif and was prominently depicted by Michelangelo in the Sistine Chapel" (Wilcox & Whitham, 2004, p. 311). "This emblem, the brass serpent, greatly influenced the 16th century renaissance of the classical Aesculapius and his attribute, the rod and serpent," when humanism influenced several long-standing motifs (Wilcox & Whitham, 2004, p. 311; citing Schouten, J.).

Interestingly, "this symbol is known as the Tau cross and is featured on the coat of arms of the royal Society of Medicine of the United Kingdom, where it is often mistaken for an Asklepian" (Wilcox & Whitham, 2004, p. 311).

In Eastern cultures, the staff is also "viewed as a type of... cosmic axis connecting this world with the underworld and the heavens" (Williams, 1999, p. 475). Asklepios's staff, for instance, assisted this Greek god of health in his "wanderings to serve humankind" (Williams, 1999, p. 475). According to the earliest known writings, dating from approximately 1500 BC, Asklepios (known by his more familiar Roman name, Aesculapius) was considered to be the son of Apollo and his mortal mistress Coronis (Stanton, 1999). Aesculapius assumed the form of a serpent to deliver a city from the plague. Those who suffered were healed when licked by snakes in his temples.

Curiously, blood from the right side of the Gorgon, a female creature with sharp fangs and hair of living, venomous snakes, gave Aesculapius the power of resurrection, while blood from her left side was fatal (Williams, 1999). Aesculapius came to be known as the healer in ancient Greek society, and later throughout the Roman Empire (Stanton, 1999).

Although the single-entwined staff of Asklepios is the most popular symbol of medicine internationally, the "medical caduceus" has become the more popular symbol in the United States today. This symbol consists of a double serpent-entwined staff with surmounting wings (see illustration at the beginning of this chapter) and is equated with the ancient caduceus, the double serpent-entwined staff of the Greco-Roman god Hermes. In their paper titled, "The Symbol of Modern Medicine: Why One Snake is More Than Two," Robert A. Wilcox and Emma M. Whitham (2003) argue that the United States medical caduceus actually has a more modern origin, and that being associated with Hermes, is inappropriate for many reasons (Wilcox & Whitham, 2003). However, upon reflection on the duality evi-

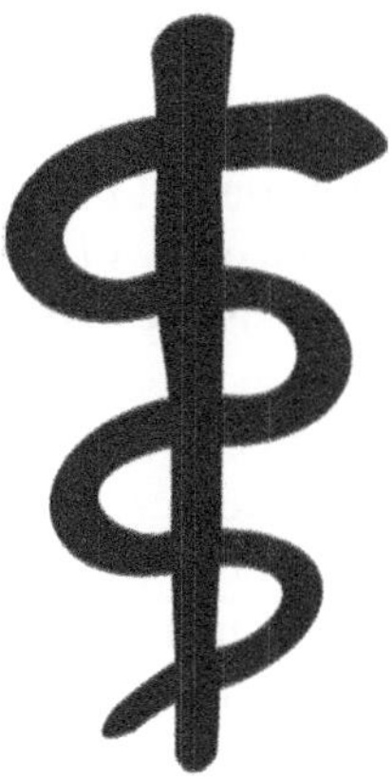

Staff of Aesculapius. Courtesy of Wikimedia Commons.

dent in the field of medicine and its international symbol, the caduceus of Hermes appears to be precisely appropriate.

Hermes, the son of Zeus and the nymph Maia, is the herald of the Olympian gods; the god of boundaries and the travelers who cross them. He is also considered a messenger from the gods to humans. In fact, we derive the word "hermeneutics" from this god, signifying the art of interpreting hidden meaning. In a field with origins to the healing arts, where "mystical powers as well as practical applications" (Williams, 1999, p. 475) are attributed to its symbols, one wonders if Hermes is in fact a very appropriate god to associate with the field of medicine.

Wilcox and Whitham (2003) argue that Hermes would not be appropriate due to his reputation for being "overly shrewd" and cunning, as well as for being considered "the guide of souls along the pathways to the underworld." Yet serpents, with their ability to heal or destroy, have also been associated with both the heavens and the underworld. This theme of duality and the struggle between good and evil, death and life, appears constant throughout the field of medicine.

In medical journals, doctors argue for a reminder to always uphold one's profession with utmost dignity and respect in order to gain and keep the respect of one's patients and society as a whole. This presents another struggle. Judith Anne Stanton (1999) notes, "although people in the United States have access to more technologically advanced healthcare than ever before, they are more distrustful of doctors and the powers of what may be broadly called the 'medical system'" (p. 476), thus leaving doctors to bear "the same social burden of both veneration and hostility" (p. 477).

This dualism thus also symbolizes an inner struggle within ourselves "to reconcile conflicting desires and beliefs... about our own mortality," leaving doctors with the challenging task of "carefully negotiating the contradictions of the powers and limits" inherent in saving lives (Stanton, 1999, p. 477).

In conclusion, although the conflict between which symbol is most appropriate (Asklepios vs. the caduceus), or which symbols to use in grading systems (Schunemann, Best, Vist, & Oxman, 2003) may not be solved tomorrow, one thing remains clear: literacy, or in this case, medical symbols, is a "socially contested" concept (Lankshear, 1999, pp. 12–13, citing J. P. Gee), and the debate about literacy "ultimately comes down to moral choices about what theories one wants to hold based on the sorts of social worlds these theories underwrite in the present or make possible in the future" (Lankshear, 1999, p. 13; citing J. P. Gee).

37

Sports Literacy

Gabriel Quintana

A Football Official Signals "Touchdown." Clip art courtesy of Microsoft Corporation.

Many social and cultural fields have a vocabulary that is unique to them. These vocabularies provide practical terms that are crucial in the progress and success of the activities in the field. One such example is seen in the world of sports.

The vocabulary of sports can be broken down into three interrelated categories: the rules, the inward aspects, and the outward aspects. The

Multiliteracies: Beyond Text and the Written Word, pages 171–174

rules include the definitions, the procedure of play, and the official signals; knowledge of specific plays and sportsmanship encompass the inner aspects of sports; the outer aspects of sports include the residuals of the game, both positive and negative, such as knowledge of gambling terms and cultural affinity and dependence. In this chapter we will examine each of the major sports in American society and describe the literacies that promote the success of these sports.

The first sport for commentary is American football, arguably the most popular game in the United States. In American football, players attempt to advance the ball from one side of the rectangular field to another. To accomplish this, the knowledge of certain terms, such as "forward pass," "touchdown," and "field goal," is essential. Further, successfully advancing the ball is dependent on players' and coaches' knowledge of symbols in a playbook. Other literacies in football include knowledge of the signals demonstrated by the officials during the course of a game (Hanion, 1998). The game has also affected American society in many different ways, including the social gatherings during "Super Bowl Sunday" and the tradition of enjoying a football game while preparing Thanksgiving dinner.

Basketball also has its unique set of terminology. For instance, fans watching a basketball game may hear terms such as a "dunk," "dribbling," and "rebounding." Like football, players must be able to interpret the symbols in a playbook to successfully score a basket (Collvins, 2007). For those fans viewing a game in an arena, they must interpret the meanings of the

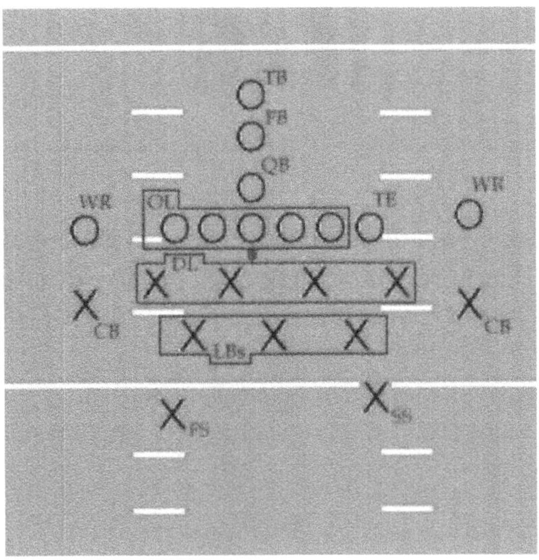

Diagram of Typical American-Football Formations. English Wikipedia 2007, January 21, 2007.

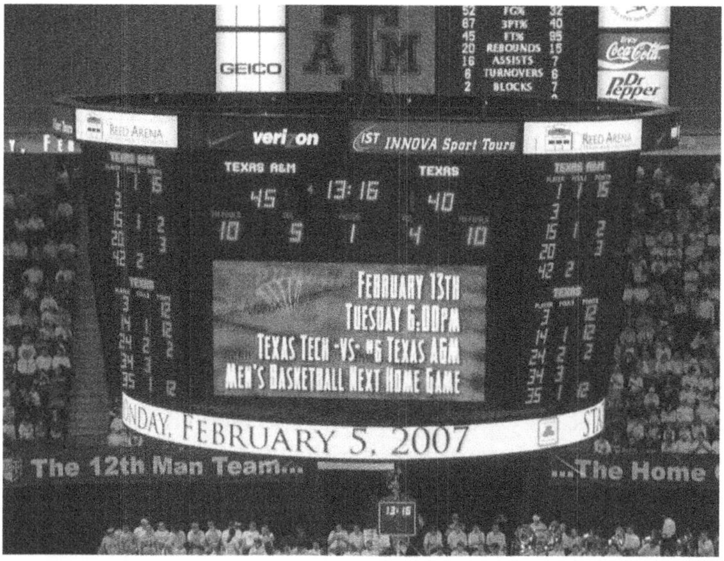

A Basketball Scoreboard. Courtesy of Wikipedia.

numbers flickering on a scoreboard, such as time remaining in the period, number of team fouls, and the score. The social arena of gambling is also affected by the terminology in basketball as well as all other sports, such as betting the "over/under" (betting that both teams will score greater or fewer points than a predetermined mark) and "winning the tip" (betting who will get possession of the ball first, which occurs after a "jump ball" or tip).

The final major American sport used as an example to demonstrate alternative literacies is baseball. Baseball marks its distinction among American

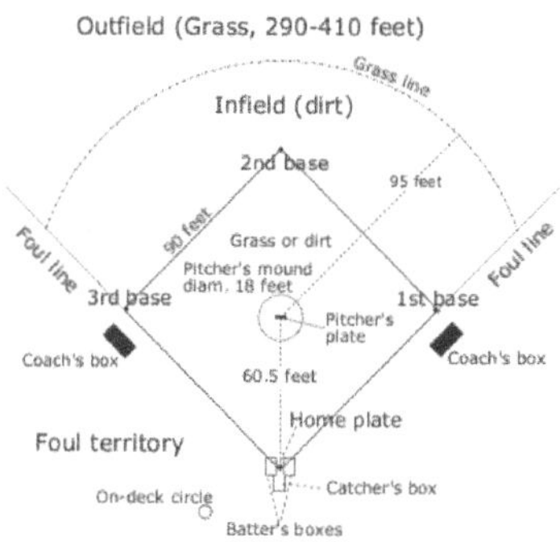

Overview of a Baseball Field. English Wikipedia 2005, October 27, 2005. Courtesy of Robert Merkel.

sports in that it is not played in a traditional rectangular field; rather it is played on a "diamond," which is a square with sides of 90 feet, and in an extended field, called the "outfield." Hence, even the layout of the field requires its own literacy. The game itself has its own terminology, including "base on balls," "infield fly rule," and "balk" (Major League Baseball, 1999). Further, the sport's societal influence is extremely important, earning it the nickname "America's National Pastime."

What do these sports terminologies tell us about the nature of certain literacies? First is their necessity for the success of American sports. Time and again, we see how the three categories outlined earlier interrelate with each other—each sport has its own rules, inward aspects, and the outward aspects. Although some of these categories of sports literacies consist of complex elements, they are all employed and learned in an informal way. In this context, an important characteristic of alternative or multiliteracies can be seen, that is the relatively informal context in which these literacies are assimilated or learned, and the sophistication of the concepts or literacies that are at work.

38

Interpersonal Literacy through Gestures

Maribel G. Harder

In The School of Athens by Raphael, body language and gestures convey a great deal of meaning. Image courtesy of Wikimedia Commons.

The purpose of schooling, one would say, is to prepare children to become future leaders of our society. Literacy, in point of fact, is considered of prime importance to becoming successful, productive

Multiliteracies: Beyond Text and the Written Word, pages 175–179

citizens. However, when literacy is limited solely to reading and writing, the possibility of success for our children is greatly restricted to a handful of professions that do not require considerable social interaction. Yet, across various disciplines, humans have been described as social creatures, innately seeking relationships and identity with a group or various groups.

Leaders in all walks of life need strong communication skills that entail awareness of one's *nonverbal communication* via body language, eye contact, gestures, and the like. As a result, the ability to "read" people, is a slang term that may in fact shed light on an alternative literacy, which, when strong, can greatly aid an individual's chances of success in our increasingly global community.

This alternative literacy traces its beginnings back to antiquity, before language even came into existence, yet it is just as significant today as it ever has been. So significant are nonverbal modes of communication that, as mentioned earlier in this book, *emoticons* have been created to emulate face-to-face conversation and enhance the written text communication experience.

This desire to enhance written communication with cartoon facial expressions becomes even more evident when studies have found nonverbal modes of communication to serve a very "economical" purpose. This purpose is achieved when a speaker does not overload "utterances," having hands to supplement what is being said (i.e., using a single hand movement to describe the path of a motion) (Goffman, 1979). In fact, gestures have been found not only to be complimentary to one's speech, but capable of standing alone to communicate certain feelings, intentions, academic concepts, and expectations.

In 1993, Jurgen Streeck argued that "gesture" is one of the least charted terrains in human communication, partially due to the fact that it is *visual* "and has therefore not received the concentrated attention of linguists" (Streeck, J., 1993, p. 276). Throughout history, its significance is ever present. The Greeks and the Romans considered the proper delivery of "gesticulation" to be a pivotal part of good oratory.[1] Today, articles are written to share the most effective hand and body movements for outstanding lecturers to use.

In his textbook *Institutio oratoria* (1975), Quintillianus made the art of gesticulation a significant part of rhetorical instruction, citing hand-movements made during speeches 200 years before his lifetime "to illustrate the merits and flaws of different kinds of gesture" (Streeck, J., 1993, p. 277). According to Quintillianus, good style gestures were abstract motions that embellish the speech and visualize its pragmatic structure. In fact, the urban elite prized relying exclusively on language to convey truth as a demonstration of sophistication. Bad style gestures represented the content of the speech and showed what the speaker was talking about. Thus, the highest form of gesturing did not replace language or communication, but enhanced it.

These "pictorial" gestures were also believed by the Romans to be primarily for the arts, on a stage versus the orator's rostrum. Interestingly, at the dawn of the Rennaissance, gestures were included in paintings "as self-sufficient representations of the communicative act intended in the work of art," providing "the audience with important clues about the references and *meanings*" (Streeck, J., 1993, p. 277).

According to Jurgen Streeck, literature has expressed a true fascination with gesture as *symbolization*—as a nonlinguistic, yet meaningful "technology" to represent the world and our ideas about it, and to do so in ways that others, knowing the rules of the symbolisms, can understand (p. 279).[1]

In addition, this nonverbal form of communication has allowed for understanding across languages. Streeck notes that members of a Greek expedition-corps engaged in conversation with natives abroad via the use of signs they had seen deaf-mutes use. Furthermore, Columbus recorded in his journal that "gesture enabled him to freely converse and build universes of shared meaning across even the largest cultural divide" (Streeck, 1993, p. 279). Furthermore, in our postmodern era, where cultures are increasingly intermingling, the ability to "read" and express appropriate nonverbal communication is pivotal.

Studies have found that many gestures are cultural whereas others are universal. The cultural gestures serve universal functions that other communities also express via alternative nonverbal forms (Streeck, 1993).

Even within one's own culture and language, non-verbal communication plays a crucial role. Studies have shown that 60% of what we communicate occurs through our body language, whereas 30% is communicated via vocal attributes (such as rate, pitch volume and tone), with only 10% of what we "say" coming from our actual words. In fact, communication experts indicate that when the two styles are incongruent, nonverbal communication carries more impact than verbal communication (Skow & Whitaker, 1996).

Essential components of this interpersonal literacy include approachability, availability, closeness and warmth, and multi-channeled communication (with possible channels such as the body, hands, eyes, mouth, arms, surrounding space, use of time, and even the color of one's clothing). The

Christian B. Anfinsen (left), American biochemist, shaking hands with president Jimmy Carter in 1980. Courtesy of Libby Anfinsen.

nonverbal characteristics that relay these components are a relaxed stance, gestures, smiles, eye contact, and uncrossed arms.

Nonverbal communication's universality and communicative power make it intriguing and significant to our interactions. In fact, in the realm of teaching, Wolff-Michael Roth states that "gestures constitute a central feature of human development, knowing, learning, and communication across cultures" (Roth, 2001, p. 365). In an interesting study analyzing highly successful college-age tutors working with fourth grade at-risk children in a culturally diverse elementary school, Jeanne B. Cobb (2000) found that "masterful use of *body language* and *gestures* by the tutors" was "an essential part of effective listening behavior" (p. 103).

Jeanne B. Cobb further found that "these tutors used *non-verbal communication* to convey the message to the child that, 'You are the most important person in the world to me, right now, and for the next thirty minutes, you have my undivided attention" (Cobb, 2000, p. 103).

These socio-communication skills are further expanded in the literature for teachers and principals in order to be effective leaders in their schools and classrooms. Skow and Whitaker (1996) stress that being aware of what we say as well as our nonverbal cues is critical to establishing successful communication.

In fact, "there is no more essential skill for any school leader than good communication" (Skow & Whitaker, 1996, p. 3). Furthermore, using effective communication such as selecting appropriate nonverbal behaviors that can help to defuse a tense interaction is not only a necessity for individuals taking on administrative and leadership roles, but for anyone who desires to communicate successfully with coworkers, family, loved ones, and friends.

Thus, as an alternative form of literacy, nonverbal communication or interpersonal literacy has evolved, from preceding language, to enhancing it, in a way that adds dimensionality, depth, and intrigue. Only through our awareness of this alternative form of literacy can we master it and use it effectively.

39

Electronic Books

Eugene F. Provenzo, Jr.

A Kindle screen of a front page of *The New York Times* and a front page of a paper version of the *Times*. Photograph by Eugene F. Provenzo, Jr.

Multiliteracies: Beyond Text and the Written Word, pages 181–183

We take books for granted in our day-to-day lives and rarely think of them as a technology in the way that we think of computers or cell phones. In fact, however, books are a relatively new technology dating back to the late medieval period when primitive versions of them were printed from woodblocks. The modern book, based on the technology of moveable type, was invented in about 1450 by Johannes Gutenberg.

The modern book is dramatically different from other textual devices. It is in many ways much more efficient than the ancient scroll, which was used throughout the Middle Ages, and which required one to move from beginning to end or from back to front—literally unwinding the text as one read. Referencing a specific line of text was a difficult task, since there were not clear lines or measured sections of text set off in the scroll.

The modern book superseded the scroll by incorporating a number of remarkable technologies. By the late Renaissance these included numbered pages, tables of contents, charts, indexes, italic type, bold face type, and similar types of forms. Combined with the mass circulation of books and other printed materials such as broadsheets, newspapers, and magazines, they created a revolution in literacy.

All of this suggests that what we take for granted as the fundamental tools of literacy and text are relatively recent inventions—many no more than four or five hundred years old. If we are in fact emerging into a post-typographic culture, one that is changing the meaning of textuality as dramatically as the Gutenberg Revolution changed the meaning and representation of text, then we should not be surprised that we are experiencing new forms and mechanisms of reading—just as occurred during the early Renaissance.

In the case of electronic books or e-books and e-book readers, we are seeing new textual forms rapidly come into use. Various types of e-books have existed since the late 1990s. The Franklin eBookMan, for example, was introduced in 1999, about the same time as the RocketEbook. These early devices used LCD screens. E-paper technology imitates the appearance of ink on paper. Rather than using a backlight display typical of LCD devices, e-paper uses charged pigment particles (white and black) suspended in oil using an applied electric field. The result is a highly readable text in black and white, which requires minimal power to operate.

In 2006 Sony introduced it Sony Reader an e-book reader based on this technology. The following year Amazon.com introduced a similar device called the Kindle. As of April 2008, the Kindle had access to over 110,000 books, blogs, magazines, and newspapers. Using the same connectivity as cell phones, the Kindle makes it possible to download a book in less than sixty seconds.

The Kindle, which weighs about ten ounces and is roughly the size of a small paperback book, does many things a traditional book cannot do. As Jeff Bezos, the founder of Amazon.Com explains:

> If you come across a word you don't recognize, you can look it up easily. You can search your books. Your margin notes and underlining are stored on the server-side in the "cloud," where they can't be lost. Kindle keeps your place in each of the books you're reading automatically. If your eyes are tired, you can change the font size. (Bezos, 2008)

Bezos is acutely aware that the Kindle and e-books represent a revolution. Unlike devices like the Blackberry, which can also handle long text documents, the Kindle is designed for sustained reading of long texts such as novels and full-length histories. The device makes large numbers of books available almost instantly. Accessibility is changed, and new models of commerce production become possible. Books no longer need to be printed and warehoused. The secondhand market for books is eliminated. In the case of college textbook publishers, books can have their price drastically reduced by eliminating the secondhand book market and many of their shipping and distribution costs. Books can be easily and inexpensively updated. In addition, audio functions can be added to the book with its MP3 player. Although still in its experimental stages, it is clear that e-readers like the Kindle will make it possible to have a book read aloud to you while you read it, or to have sounds accompany the text.

What happens when a French textbook can have its vocabulary repeated by a native speaker? What is it like for a book on the history of composer such as Johann Sebastian Bach to have his works played along with the text? It is not that this technology is new. It has been available on computers for some years. What makes e-books such as the Kindle different is how they make such a process practical and potentially part of our daily life.

Equally profound changes occur in the reading process. We don't know what the sociology of the e-book will be and how, in the end, it will affect people. But there is every reason to believe it will create a new model of reading and literacy, quite possibly of the same magnitude as the Gutenberg Revolution 500 years earlier.

Afterword

In works such as *The Pedagogy of the Oppressed* and *Education for Critical Consciousness*, the Brazilian educational theorist Paulo Freire argues that illiterates are considered "undernourished." According to this metaphor, illiteracy—specifically the inability to read text—involves a lack of food or sustenance. In this context, the "bread of the spirit" is provided by the ideas and information found in textual reading.

Such a model, as demonstrated by the essays included in this book, is extremely limited. Literacy operates at many levels and in many ways. Some literacies are direct offshoots of textuality, such as emoticons. Others, such as rebuses, traffic signs, and patriotic symbols, are visual code systems. Still others involve kinesthetic and tactile elements such as American Sign Language and Baby Sign Language.

What is clear is that as we emerge into a postmodern culture, literacy, and how we define it, is becoming increasingly complex, multidimensional, and integrated. The metaphor of a collage involving many different elements (text, sound, body movements, and visual symbols) comes to mind.

We recognize that oral traditions and, tactile literacies, to name a few, have always been part of being literate. But postmodern literacy—largely as a result of computing—somehow goes beyond even the expanded notions of literacy that were found in the modern period.

In this context, new modalities emerge that recall earlier traditions, but that are transformed through new technologies such as computing. Thus the modern textual tradition of letter writing, for example, is transformed

Multiliteracies: Beyond Text and the Written Word, pages 185–187

by computer-based systems such as e-mail and text messaging. Traditional oral forms are reinvented with the technology of cell phones and text messaging. New modalities make possible new literacies—literacies that often combine the old and the new.

Like the members of the New London Group, whom we cite at the beginning of this work, we believe that what we are seeing is the emergence a new type of literacy that involves multiliteracies that increasingly pervade our consciousness and understanding of the world.

As we have seen, these multiliteracies are often deeply cultural and suggest that general literacy goes far beyond the technical ability to read and decode text. Instead, the "new" literacy involves the negotiation of many modes and many ways of understanding the world.

If all that we have said above, and in the rest of this work, is true, then the question arises as to how does what we have described affect the nature of schooling and the process of teaching people to read.

In Howard Gardner's theory of multiple intelligences, he describes seven different types of intelligence: linguistic, logical-mathematical, musical, bodily-kinesthetic, spatial, interpersonal, and intrapersonal. These first two types of intelligence are the ones that have typically been valued by schools, and children who possessed linguistic or logical-mathematical intelligence were considered to be "smart."

In the multiliteracies we have explored in this book, we similarly go beyond the traditional literacies that are associated with school-based literacy, namely the ability to read printed text. As we evolve into a post-modern society, multiple literacies, just like multiple intelligences, will play an increasingly important part in students' success. From being able to understand nonverbal communication such as body language, to having the required skills for using text-messaging, e-mail, and other forms of electronic communication, to interpreting the messages conveyed by classmates fashion statements, these literacies (and others) contribute to students' prospects for success in school and beyond.

In schools today, some of these literacies may be taught explicitly (such as those related to computers, or, in specific academic programs: dance literacy, American Sign Language, and numeracy and orders of magnitude), while others may be passed down through the school and the more general culture (such as the ability to interpret fashion branding, death t-shirts, or tattoos).

Are these more cultural literacies things which should be explicitly taught in school? Probably not in most cases, but they are important literacies which may merit discussion in secondary school social studies programs in order to broaden students' cultural awareness and understanding. In contrast to Friere's definition of literacy discussed earlier, the United Nations Educational Scientific and Cultural Organization (UNESCO) has defined literacy in the following way:

> Literacy is the ability to identify, understand, interpret, create, communicate, compute and use printed and written materials associated with varying contexts. Literacy involves a continuum of learning to enable an individual to achieve his or her goals, to develop his or her knowledge and potential, and to participate fully in the wider society. (Anton & Nelson, 2006)

This definition fits more closely with the challenges faced by people in a postmodern society, and, we believe, highlights the importance of the multiliteracies covered in this book.

References

Abraham, R. (2002). *History of fractal geometry.* Retrieved March 30, 2007, from http://www.visual-chaos.org/complexity/branches/fractals.html.

Abram, S. (2008). Did you hear that? The internet firmament is shifting. *MultiMedia Internet Sch, 15,* 27.

Acredolo, L., Goodwyn, S., & Abrams, D. (2002). *Baby signs: How to talk with your baby before your baby can talk.* New York: McGraw-Hill.

Acredolo, L. & Goodwyn, S. (2000). The long-term impact of symbolic gesturing during infancy on IQ at Age 8. *Paper presented at the meetings of the International Society for Infant Studies,* Brighton, UK.

Adams, R. J. (2007). *American flag.* Retrieved Mar 1, 2007, from http://www.awesomelibrary.org/Classroom/Social_Studies/History/American_History/American_Flag.html.

Akamatsu, C.T., Mayer, C. & Farrelly, S. (2006). An investigation of two-way text messaging use with deaf students at the secondary level. *Journal of Deaf Studies and Deaf Education, 11*(1), 120–131.

Arnove, R. F. & Graff, H.J. (2001). National literacy campaigns. In E. Cushman, E. Kintgen, B. Kroll, and M. Rose (Eds.). *Literacy: A Critical Sourcebook* (pp. 591–615). New York: Bedford/St. Martins.

Baer, J. W. (1992). *The pledge of allegiance: A short history.* Retrieved Mar 10, 2007, from http://history.vineyard.net/pledge.htm.

Baldaev, D. (Ed.). (2004). *Russian criminal tattoo encyclopedia, Vol. I.* London: Fuel.

Baldaev, D. (Ed.). (2006) *Russian criminal tattoo encyclopedia, Vol. II.* London: Fuel.

Baldrige, L. (1990). *Complete guide to the new manners for the '90s.* New York: Rawson Associates.

Baker, C. (1996). *Your genes, your choices: Exploring the issues raised by genetic research.* Washington, DC: American Association for the Advancement of Science.

Multiliteracies: Beyond Text and the Written Word, pages 189–200

Bartlett, J. (1968). *Bartlett's familiar quotations, fourteenth edition.* Boston: Little, Brown.

Battison, R., (2001). *Analyzing signs in linguistics of American sign language: An introduction by Clayton Valli.* Washington, DC: Gallaudet University Press.

Baudrillard, J. (1983). *Simulations* (Paul Foos, Paul Patton, & Philip Beitchman. Trans). New York: Semiotext(e)

Baur, S., Percevic, R., Okon, E., Meermann, R., & Kordy, H. (2003). Use of text messaging in the aftercare of patients with bulimia nervosa. *European Eating Disorders Review, 11*(3), 279–290.

Beckmann, S. (2005). *Mathematics for elementary teachers.* Upper Saddle River, NJ: Pearson Education.

Bezos, J. P. (2008). *Letter to share owners: April, 2008.* Seattle, Washington.

Bowe, F. G. (2002). Deaf and hard of hearing Americans' instant messaging and e-mail use: A national survey. *American Annals of the Deaf, 147*(4), 6–10.

Branding. (2004). *Merriam-Webster Online Dictionary.* Retrieved April 4, 2008, from http://www.merriam-webster.com.

Brecht, S. (1988). *The bread and puppet theatre: l and II.* London: Routledge, Chapman and Hall.

Breneman, J. A. (2005). *America's quilting history, Hmong needlework: Traditions both ancient and new.* Retrieved March 4, 2007, from http://www.womenfolk.com/quilting_history/hmong.htm.

Bush, V. (1945). As we may think. *Atlantic Monthly, 176*(1), 101–108.

Cella, D. F., & others. (1992). Culturally relevant smoking prevention for minority youth. *Journal of School Health, 62*(8), 377–380.

Cha, D. (1996). *Dia's story cloth.* New York: Lee and Low.

Cho, H. (27 August, 2006). The *Baltimore Sun* On the Job column: The power of the thank-you note. *Knight Ridder Tribune Business News.* Retrieved February 29, 2008, from ABI/INFORM Complete database. (Document ID: 1326081401).

Clark, J. & Franzmann, M. (2006). Authority from grief, presence and place in the making of roadside memorials. *Death Studies, 30,* 581–595.

Clay, M. (1993). *An observation survey of early literacy achievement.* Portsmouth, NH: Heinemann.

CNBC ticker. (2007). Retrieved February 1, 2007, from http://en.wikipedia.org/wiki/CNBC_Ticker.

Collins, A. (2002). *Learning science and the science of learning.* Arlington, VA: National Science Teachers Association Press.

Collins, C. O., & Rhine, C. D. (2003). Roadside memorials. *Omega, 47*(3), 221–222.

Collvins, L. (2007). *Basketball site.* Retrieved March 14, 2007, from http://www.bellaonline.com/articles/art1370.asp.

Computer simulation. (2008). Retrieved March 11, 2008, from http://en.wikipedia.org/wiki/Computer_simulation.

Conklin, J. (1987). Hypertext: An introduction and survey. *Computer, 20*(9), 17–41.

Crossley, J. N. (1987). *The emergence of number.* Singapore: World Scientific.

Critchley, M. (1970). *The language of gesture.* Folcroft, PA: Folcroft Printing.

Cushman, E., Kintgen, E. R., Kroll, B. M., & Rose, M. (Eds.). (2001). *Literacy: A critical sourcebook.* New York: Bedford/St. Martins.

Dao, Y. (2007). *Hmong American partnership.* Retrieved March 3, 2007, from http://www.hmong.org.

Darwin, C. (1872). *The expression of the emotions in man and animals.* London: John Murray.

Davies, E., (2001). *Beyond dance: Laban's legacy of movement analysis.* New York: Routledge.

Deaf Culture. (2008). Retrieved on April 10, 2008, from http://www.aslinfo.com/deafculture.cfm.

De Mello, M. (2000). *Bodies of inscription: A cultural history of the modern tattoo community.* Durham, NC: Duke University Press.

Department of the Navy. (2006). *Origin of navy terminology.* Retrieved February 23, 2007, from http://www.history.navy.mil/library/online/origin.htm#kno.

Dibra, B., & Crenshaw, M. A. (1999). *Dogspeak.* New York: Fireside.

Dobbins, K. W. (2005). Getting ready for the net generation learner. *EDUCAUSE Review, 40*(5), 8–9.

Doyle, B. (2004). Road signs. *US Catholic, 69*(8), 49.

Duke, N.K. & Purcell-Gates, V. (2003). Genres at home and at school: Bridging the known to the new. *The Reading Teacher, 57*(1), 30–37.

DuPont, M. K. (1998). *Business etiquette and professionalism: Your guide to career success.* Menlo Park, CA: Course Technology Crisp.

Ekman, P., & Friesen, W. V. (1970). Constants across cultures in the face and emotion. *Journal of Personality and Social Psychology, 17,* 124–129.

Ekman, P., Sorenson, R. E., & Friesen, W. V. (1969). Pan-cultural elements in facial displays of emotions. *Science, 164,* 86–88.

Emoticons. (2006). Retrieved February 7, 2007, from http://en.wikipedia.org/wiki/Emoticons.

Etiquette. (2006). *The American Heritage® Dictionary of the English Language, Fourth Edition,* retrieved February 29, 2008, from http://dictionary.reference.com/browse/etiquette.

Eves, H. (1990). *Foundations and fundamental concepts of mathematics* (3rd ed.). Mineola, NY: Dover Publications, Inc.

Facebook factsheet. (2008). Retrieved April 10, 2008, from Facebook Web site: www.facebook.com/press/info.php?factsheet.

Fashions for December. (1842). *Ladies world of fashion,* 2(6), 2.

Forbis, M. (1994). *This is my body: Gender, tattooing and resistance in the United States. A thesis submitted to the Temple University Graduate Board.* Retrieved

March 11, 2008, from http://astro.temple.edu/~ruby/wava/forbis/forbis-title.html.

Freire, P. (2001). The adult literacy process as cultural action for freedom and education and conscientizacao. In E. Cushman, E. Kintgen, B. Kroll, & M. Rose (Eds.). *Literacy: A critical sourcebook* (pp. 616–628). New York: Bedford/St. Martins.

Fuller, R. B. (1984). Foreword. In H. Dreyfuss, *Symbol sourcebook: An authoritative guide to international graphic symbols* (pp. 14–15). New York: John Wiley and Sons. Retrieved February 25, 2007, from http://books.google.com/books?id=HwSVn2PZCSAC.

Garcia, H. (2002). Poetics and aesthetics of violence in tattoos. Retrieved March 19, 2008, from http://bad.eserver.org/issues/2002/62/garcia.html.

Gardner, H. (1993). *Multiple intelligences: New horizons in theory and practice.* New York: Basic Books.

Garrison, D. R., Anderson, T., & Archer, W. (1999). Critical inquiry in a text-based environment: Computer conferencing in higher education. *The Internet and Higher Education, 2*(2–3), 87–105.

Gaur, A. (1987). *A history of writing.* London: British Library. Original work published in 1984.

Gazale, M. (2000). *Number: From Ahmes to Cantor.* Princeton, NJ: Princeton University Press.

Gee, J. P. (1996). *Social linguistics and literacies: Ideology in discourses.* London: Falmer.

Giving Signals. (2008). Retrieved April 2, 2008, from http://www.baseball.ca/eng_doc.cfm?DocID=108&Related=17.

GLINN Media & Schramm, D. (n.d.). *The quilt weekend—Rage against the dying of the light: never surrender, never forget.* Retrieved February 12, 2007, from http://www.ragefilm.com.

Goffman, E. (1988). *Gender advertisements.* New York: Harper-Collins.

Goodwyn, S., Acredolo, L., & Brown, C. (2000). Impact of symbolic gesturing on early language development. *Journal of Nonverbal Behavior, 24*(2), 83–101.

Goodwyn, S., & Acredolo, L. (1993). Symbolic gesture versus word: Is there a modality advantage for onset of symbol ise? *Child Development, 64,* 698.

Goody, J. (2001). What's in a list? In E. Cushman, E. R. Kintgen, B.M. Kroll, & M. Rose (Eds.), *Literacy: A critical sourcebook* (pp. 32–51). Boston: Bedfod/St. Martin's.

Graff, H.J. (1995). *The labyrinths of literacy: Reflections on literacy past and present, Revised and expanded edition.* Pittsburgh, PA: University of Pittsburgh Press.

Graffiti. (n.d.). *Online etymology dictionary.* Retrieved April 12, 2007, from Dictionary.com website: http://dictionary.reference.com/browse/graffiti.

Groce, N., (1985). *Everyone here spoke sign language: Hereditary deafness on Martha's Vineyard.* Cambridge: Harvard University Press.

Guensburg, C. (1996, June 16). The fabric of their lives. *Milwaukee Journal Sentinel*, Retrieved March 3, 2007, from http://www.hmongnet.org/culture/pandau.html.

Hanion, T. W. (1998). *The sports rules book.* Champaign, IL: Human Kinetics.

Harrington, T., (2006). *Sign languages of the world, by name.* Retrieved April 10, 2008, from http://library.gallaudet.edu/deaf-faq-world-sl-name.shtml.

Hawkins, P. (1993). Naming names: The art of memory and the NAMES project AIDS quilt. *Critical Inquiry, 19*(4), 752–779.

Heath, S. B. (2001). Protean shapes in literacy events: Ever-shifting oral and literate traditions. In E. Cushman, E. Kintgen, B. Kroll, & M. Rose (Eds.), *Literacy: A critical sourcebook* (pp. 443–466). Boston: Bedford/St. Martin's.

Heath, S. B. (1978). *Outline guide for the ethnographic study of literacy and oral language from school to community.* Philadelphia: Graduate School of Education.

History of measurement. (2008). Retrieved February, 8, 2008, from http://en.wikipedia.org/wiki/History_of_measurement.

Hong, T. (2000). *Developing dance literacy in the postmodern: An approach to curriculum.* Paper presented at Dancing in the Millenium: An International Conference, Washington, DC.

Hopper, V. F. (2000). *Medieval number symbolism: Its sources, meaning, and influence on thought and expression.* New York: Dover Publications.

Horner, S. L. (2005) Categories of environmental print: All logos are not created equal. *Early Childhood Education Journal, 33*(2), 113–119.

Hough, S. E. (2007). *Richter's scale: Measure of an earthquake, measure of a man.* Princeton, NJ: Princeton University Press.

Hughes, T. (2002). Roadside tributes raise safety issue; Traffic: The memorials help ease families' pain, but officials fear people gathered at accident sites such as the one as the one near Camarillo could get hit. *Los Angeles Times, Apr 7,* B.1.

Human Genome Project Information. (2007a). Ethical, legal, and social issues. Retrieved May 14, 2008, from http://www.ornl.gov/sci/techresources/Human_Genome/elsi/elsi.shtml.

Human Genome Project Information. (2007b). Genetically modified foods and organisms. Retrieved May 14, 2008, from http://www.ornl.gov/sci/techresources/Human_Genome/elsi/gmfood.shtml.

Illman, P. E. (1995). *The pilot's handbook of aeronautical knowledge* (3rd ed.). New York: TAB Books.

In Fat Herb's Death There can be Life. (1999, October 29). *Afro-American Red Star,* Sec. A, p. 5.

Instant messaging and messengers. (2008). Retrieved February 7, 2008, from http://en.wikipedia.org/wiki/Instant_message.

Izard, C.E. (1971). *The face of emotion.* New York: Appleton-Century-Crofts.

Jackson, D., Paul, P., & Smith, J. (1997). Prior knowledge and reading comprehension ability of deaf adolescents. *Journal of Deaf Studies and Deaf Education, 2*(3), 172–184.

Jacobs, G. E. (2004). Complicating contexts: Issues of methodology in researching the language and literacies of instant messaging. *Reading Research Quarterly, 39*(4), 394–406.

Janik, V.K. & Nelson, E.S. (1998). *Fools and jesters in literature, art, and history: A bio-bibliographical sourcebook.* Westport, CT: Greenwood Press.

Jeremiah, M. A. (1992). Rap lyrics: Instruments for language arts instruction. *Western Journal of Black Studies, 16*(2), 98–102.

Jones, V. A. (1999). The white coat: Why not follow suit? *The Journal of the American Medical Association, 281*(5), 478.

Joyce, M. (1995). *Of two minds: Hypertext pedagogy and politics.* Ann Arbor: The University of Michigan Press.

Keller, D. (2004). Technological transformation, multiple literacies, and the re-visioning of education. *E-Learning, 1.* pp. 9–34.

Kershaw, B. (1992). *The Politics of Performance.* Routledge Press.

Kitwana, B. (2005). *Why white kids love hip hop.* New York: Basic Civitas Books.

Krakow, A. (1994). *Total tattoo book.* New York: Warner Book, Inc.

Kwintessential Ltd. (n.d.). *Doing business in Japan.* Retrieved February 27, 2008, from http://www.kwintessential.co.uk/etiquette/doing-business-japan.html.

Laban, R. (1966). *Choreutics.* London: MacDonald and Evans.

Lahey, T. (1999). Rejuvinating the symbols of medicine. *The Journal of the American Medical Association, 281*(5), 479.

Landow, G. P. (1989). Hypertext in literacy education, Criticism and scholarship. *Computers in the Humanities, 23,* 173.

Langford, B. Y. (2005). *Etiquette edge: The unspoken rules for business success.* Saranac Lake, NY: AMACOM.

Lankshear, C. (1999). Literacy studies in education: Disciplined developments in a post-disciplinary age. In M. Peters (Ed.), *After the disciplines.* Greenwood Press.

Lave & Wenger (1991). *Situated learning: Legitimate peripheral participation.* Cambridge, UK: Cambridge University Press.

Lee, C. (2002). Literacy practices in computer-mediated communication in Hong Kong. *Reading Matrix: An International Online Journal,* 2(2).

Lemke, J. L. (1998). MetaMedia literacy: Transforming meanings and media. Literacy for the 21st century: Technological transformation in a post-typographic world. In D. Reinking, L. Labbo, M. McKenna, & R. Kiefer (Eds.). *Handbook of literacy and technology: Transformations in a post-typographic world* (pp. 283–301). Hillsdale, NJ: Erlbaum.

Lentini, P. (1999). The cultural politics of tattooing. *Arena Journal,* Retrieved March 13, 2008, from http://www.encyclopedia.com/doc/1G1-128599427.html.

Lewis, C., & Fabos, B. (2000). But will it work in the heartland? A response and illustration. *Journal of Adolescent & Adult Literacy, 43*(5), 462–469.

Lindsay, J. (n.d.). *The Hmong in America: A story of tragedy and hope.* Retrieved March 3, 2007, from http://www.jefflindsay.com/Hmong_tragedy.html.

Lipscomb, T., et al. (2007). Cellular phone etiquette among college students. *International Journal of Consumer Studies, 31*(1).

Literate. (2006). Dictionary.com. *The American Heritage® Dictionary of the English Language, Fourth Edition.* Houghton Mifflin Company, 2004, retrieved February 10, 2008, from http://dictionary.reference.com/browse/literate.

Logos. (2007). Retrieved February 7, 2007, from http://en.wikipedia.org/wiki/Logo.

Ludins, G. H. (1980). *Seamanship for new skippers* (3rd ed.). Miami: Banyan Books.

Lugliani, G. (1996). *The quilt in the capital. In body positive.* Retrieved April 19, 2008, from http://www.thebody.com/content/art/art30264.html.

Mac Phee, J., & Reuland, E. (2007). *Realizing the impossible: Art against authority.* Oakland, CA: AK Press.

MacArthur, J. (2008). *The eagle, Ben Franklin, and the turkey.* Retrieved Mar 1, 2007, from http://www.greatseal.com/symbols/turkey.html.

MacGillivray, L. & Curwen, M.S. (2007). Tagging as a social literacy practice. *Journal of Adolescent and Adult Literacy, 50*(5), 354–369.

Major League Baseball. (1999). *1999 official rules of Major League Baseball.* Chicago: Triumph Books.

Maloney, E. S. (1999). *Chapman piloting: Seamanship & small boat handling* (63rd ed.). New York: Hearst Marine Books.

Manning, M. (2004). A world of words. *Teaching PreK–8, 34*(7), 78–79.

Manusov, V. & Patterson, M. L. (Eds.). (2006). *The SAGE handbook of nonverbal communication.* London: SAGE Publications.

Marzano, R.J. (1998). *A theory-based meta-analysis of research on instruction.* Aurora, CO: Mid-continent Research for Education and Learning.

Marzano, R.J., Gaddy, B.B., & Dean, C. (2000). *What works in classroom instruction.* Aurora, CO: Mid-continent Research for Education and Learning.

McAnear, A. (2005). The best defense is a good offense: keep the focus on knowledge generation and communication. *Learning and Leading with Technology, 32*(7), 4.

McHenry, E. & Heath, S. B. (2001). The literate and the literary: African Americans as writers and readers—1830–1940. In E. Cushman, E. Kintgen, B. Kroll, and M. Rose (Eds.), *Literacy: A critical sourcebook* (pp. 261–274). New York: Bedford/St. Martins.

Menninger, K. (1992). *Number words and number symbols: A cultural history of numbers.* New York: Dover Publications.

Mogg, K. (2000). *A short history of radical puppetry.* Retrieved March 3, 2008, from http://www.geocities.com/pract_history/puppet.html.

Moje, E. (2000). To be part of the story: The literacy practices of gangsta adolescents. *Teachers College Record, 102*(3), 651–690.

Moreland, C. (1998). *Phrases with origins.* Retrieved February 23, 2007, from http://members.aol.com/MorelandC/HaveOrigins.htm.

Nakamura, K. (2002). *About Japanese sign language.* Retrieved 2/13/08, from http://www.deaflibrary.org/jsl.html.

NAMES Project Foundation. (n.d.). *NAMES project foundation—AIDS memorial quilt.* Retrieved February 11, 2007, from http://www.aidsquilt.org/history.htm.

NAMES Project AIDS Memorial Quilt. (n.d.). Retrieved February 11, 2007, from http://www.answers.com/topic/names-project-aids-memorial-quilt.

NASA Online: Computer Simultations. (2008). Retrieved April 1, 2008, from http://www.knowitall.org/nasa/simulations/.

National Dog Bite Prevention Week. (2007). Retrieved April 10, 2008, from http://www.cdc.gov/ncipc/duip/biteprevention.htm.

National Research Council. (1996). *National science education standards.* Washington, DC: National Academy Press.

Neville, R., Greene, A., McLeod, J., Tracy, A., & Surie, J. (2002). Mobile phone text messaging can help young people manage asthma. *BMJ, 325*(7364), 600.

New London Group. (1996). A pedagogy of multiliteracies: Designing social futures. *Harvard Educational Review, 66,* 60–93.

News ticker. (2007). Retrieved March 11, 2007, from http://en.wikipedia.org/wiki/News_ticker.

O'Hanlon, C. (2007). If you can't beat 'em, join 'em. *T H E Journal, 34*(8), 38–39.

O'Sullivan, M. (2005). Emotional intelligence and deception detection: Why most people can't "read" others, but a few can. In R. E. Riggio & R. S. Feldman (Eds.), *Applications of nonverbal communication,* (pp. 215–253). Mahwah, NJ: Erlbaum.

Obermayer, J. L., Riley, W. T., & Jean-Mary, J. (2004). College smoking-cessation using cell phone text messaging. *Journal of American College Health, 53*(2), 71.

Olson, D.R. (2001). Writing and the mind. In E. Cushman, E. Kintgen, B. Kroll, & M. Rose (Eds.), *Literacy: A critical sourcebook* (pp. 107–122). Boston: Bedford/St. Martin's.

Ong, W.J. (2001). Writing is a technology that restructures thought. In E. Cushman, E. Kintgen, B. Kroll, & M. Rose (Eds.), *Literacy: A critical sourcebook* (pp. 19–31). Boston: Bedford/St. Martin's.

Parker, R. S., Hermans, C. M., & Schaefer, A. D. (2004). Fashion consciousness of Chinese, Japanese and American teenagers. *Journal of Fashion Marketing and Management, 8*(2), 176.

Paul, D. G. (2000). Rap and orality: Critical media literacy, pedagogy, and cultural synchronization. *Journal of Adolescent & Adult Literacy, 44*(3), 246–251.

Peterson, S. (1988). Translating experience and the reading of a story cloth. *The Journal of American Folklore, 101*(399), 6–22.

Piro, J.M. (2002). The picture of reading: Deriving meaning in literacy through image. *The Reading Teacher, 56*(2), 126–134.

Pither, S. S. (2002). *The complete book of numbers: The power of number symbols to shape reality.* St. Paul, MN: Llewellyn Publications.

Post, E. (1922). *Etiquette in society, in business, in politics and at home.* New York: Funk & Wagnalls, retrieved February 29, 2008, from www.bartleby.com/95/.

Powell, C. T. (1991). Rap music: An education with a beat from the street. *Journal of Negro Education, 60*(3), 245–259.

Powers, R. (2008). Recruiting in 'Facebook nation.' *BizEd, 7*(2), 64.

Provenzo, E. F. (2008 in press). *The analytical engine: Computers, knowledge and the transformation of learning.* Albany, NY: State University of New York Press.

Provenzo, E. F. (1984). Educational and the iconography of the republic: Patriotic symbolism in the frontispieces of eighteenth- and nineteenth-century American textbooks. *Teachers College Record, 85,* 503–512.

Purcell-Gates, V. (2001). A world without print. In E. Cushman, E. Kintgen, B. Kroll, & M. Rose (Eds.), *Literacy: A critical sourcebook* (pp. 402–417). New York: Bedford/St. Martins.

Ramirez, J. D., Wiley, T. G., Klerk, G. D., Lee, E., & Wright, W. E. (2005). *Ebonics: The Urban Education Debate.* Towbridge, UK: The Cromwell Press Ltd.

Rapping. (2008). Retrieved February 4, 2008, from http://en.wikipedia.org/wiki/Rapping.

Read, B. (2004). Have you 'Facebooked' him? *The Chronicle of Higher Education, 50,* A29.

Reid, J. & Reid, C. (2001). A cross marks the spot: A study of roadside death memorials in Texas and Oklahoma. *Death Studies, 25,* 350.

Reisel, M. (n.d.). *Laban's legacy.* Retreived March 10, 2008 from http://www.labanproject.com/bios.html.

Remland, M. S. (2000). *Nonverbal communication in everyday life.* Boston, MA: Houghton Mifflin Company.

Repman, J., Zinskie, C., & Carlson, R. D. (2005). Effective use of CMC tools in interactive online learning. *Computers in the Schools, 22*(1–2), 57–69.

Rezabeck, L.L., & Cochenour, J.J. (1995, October). *Emoticons: Visual cues for computer-mediated communication.* Paper presented at the Annual Conference of the International Visual Literacy Association October 12–16, 1994.

Rickford, J. (2003). What is Ebonics (African American Vernacular English)? *Linguistic Society of America.* Retrieved February 29, 2008, from http://www.lsadc.org/info/ling-faqs-ebonics.cfm.

Rickford, J. & Rickford, R. (2000). *Spoken soul: The story of Black English.* [Electronic Version]. Retrieved February 29, 2008, from http://media.wiley.com/product_data/excerpt/6X/04713235/047132356X.pdf.

Rose, T. (1991). Fear of a black planet: Rap music and black cultural politics in the 1990s. *Journal of Negro Education, 60*(3), 276–290.

Ross, B. D. (1985). *Iwo Jima: Legacy of valor.* New York: Vanguard.

Ross, J. & Harradine, R. (2004). I'm not wearing that! Branding and young children. *Journal of Fashion Marketing and Management, 8*(1), 12–21.

Rubba, J. (1997) *Ebonics: Q & A.* [Electronic Version]. Retrieved February 29, 2008, from http://cla.calpoly.edu/~jrubba/Ebonics.html.

Ruetzel, D.R., Fawson, P.C., Young, J.R., Morrison, T.G., & Wilcox, B. (2003). Reading environmental print: What is the role of concepts about print in discriminating young readers' responses? *Reading Psychology, 24*(2), 123–162.

Rush, L.S. (2003). Taking a broad view of literacy: Lessons from the Appalachian Trail thru-hiking community. *Reading Online, 6*(7).

Rusin, D. (2000). *A gentle introduction to the mathematics subject classification scheme.* Retrieved March 30, 2007, from http://www.math.niu.edu/~rusin/known-math/index/beginners.html.

Sabath, A. M. (2002). *Business etiquette: 101 ways to conduct business with charm and savvy.* Franklin Lakes, NJ: Career Press.

Sanders, B. (1995). *A is for Ox: The collapse of literacy and the rise of violence in an electronic age.* New York: Vintage Books.

Saunders, R. H. (1999). Teaching rap: The politics of race in the classroom. *Journal of Geography, 98*(4), 185–188.

Schimmel, A. (1994). *The mystery of numbers.* Oxford Unversity Press.

Schunemann, H.J., Best, D., Vist, G., & Oxman, A.D. (2003). Letters, numbers, symbols and words: How to communicate grades of evidence and recommendations. *Canadian Medical Association, 169*(7), 677–680.

Segerstrale, U. & Molnar, P. (Eds.). (1997). *Nonverbal communication: Where nature meets culture.* Mahwah, NJ: Lawrence Erlbaum Associates.

Sensenbaugh, R. (1990). *Multiplicities of Literacies in the 1990s.* Bloomington, IN: ERIC Clearinghouse on Reading and Communication Skills (ED 320138). Retrieved February 15, 2008, from http://chiron.valdosta.edu/whuitt/files/literate.html.

Shreve, J. (2007). *A fitting memorial: The growing popularity of the memorial T-Shirt* [Magazine online], Retrieved March, 28, 2007, from http://www.slate.com/id2087407.

Skow, L., & Whitaker, T. (1996). It's what you say and what you do! Nonverbal immediacy behaviors: A key to effective communication. *NASSP Bulletin, 80*(584), 90–95.

Soanes, C., & Stevenson, A. (Eds.) (2004). *Concise Oxford English Dictionary.* New York: Oxford University Press.

Spielman, M.H. (1895). *The history of "Punch."* London: Cassell and Company.

Spires, H.A., & Estes, T. (2002). Reading in Web-based learning environments. In C.C. Block & M. Pressley (Eds.), *Comprehension instruction: Research-based best practices.* New York: Guilford.

Standage, T. (1999). *The Victorian Internet.* New York: Berkley Books.

Stanton, J. A. (1999). Aesculapius: A modern tale. *The Journal of the American Medical Association, 281*(5), 476–477.

Stone, L. (2003). Sign language: The art of baseball communication: The secrecy of relaying messages among players, coaches and manages is vital to the game's lifeblood. *Baseball Digest, August.*

Stull, G. (2001). The AIDS memorial quilt: Performing memory, piecing action. *American Art, 15*(2), 84–89.

Szwed, J. F. (2001). The ethnography of literacy. In E. Cushman, E. R. Kintgen, B. Kroll, & M. Rose (Eds.), *Literacy: A critical sourcebook* (p. 422). Boston: Bedford/St. Martin's.

Thompson, G. (2004). *Through ebony eyes.* San Francisco, CA: John Wiley & Sons.

Texley, S., & DeGennaro, D. (2005). Should we ban instant messaging in school? *Learning and Leading with Technology, 32*(7), 6–8.

Toppel Career Center. (2007). *Cover letters.* retrieved March 1, 2008, from http://www6.miami.edu/UMH/CDA/UMH_Main/0,1770,31647-1;54840-2;56952-3,00.html.

Traffic signs. (2007). Retrieved March 3, 2007, from http://en.wikipedia.org/wiki/Traffic_signs.

Tyson, E. H. (2002). Hip hop therapy: An exploratory study of a rap music intervention with at-risk and delinquent youth. *Journal of Poetry Therapy, 15*(3), 131–144.

Union Internationale de la Marionette (UNIMA). Retrieved March 4, 2008, from http://www.unimasa.org/about/index.html.

Virtual AIDS Quilt. (n.d.). Retrieved February 11, 2007, from http://www.virtualaidsquilt.org.

Visoná, M. B. (2005). Redefining twentieth century African art: The view from the lagoons of Côte d'Ivoire. *African Arts, 38,* 54.

Vygotsky, L. (1978). *Mind in society: The development of higher psychological processes.* Cambridge, MA. Harvard University Press.

Walther, J.B., & D'Addario. (2001). The impacts of emoticons on message interpretation in computer-mediated communication. *Social Science Computer Review, 19,* 324–347. Retrieved February 4, 2007, from: http://ssc.sagepub.com/cgi/content/abstract/19/3/324.

Weinstein, S. (2007). A love for the thing: The pleasures of rap as a literate practice. *Journal of Adolescent & Adult Literacy, 50*(4), 270–281.

Werner, B. & Kaplan, B. (1963). *Symbol formation: An organismic–developmental approach to language and the expression of thought.* Hoboken, NJ: John Wiley & Sons, Inc.

Wilcox, R. A. & Whitham, E. M. (2004). The symbol of modern medicine. *Annals of Internal Medicine, 140*(4), 311–312.

Wilcox, R. A. & Whitham, E. M. (2003). The symbol of modern medicine: Why one snake is more than two. *Annals of Internal Medicine, 138*(8), 673–677.

Will it Ever Change? (2006, May 12). *The Broward Times,* 1.

Williams, N. W. (1999). Serpents, staffs, and the emblems of medicine. *The Journal of the American Medical Association, 281*(5), 475.

Willis, J. (2007). The gully in the "brain glitch" theory. *Educational Leadership, 64*(5), 68–73.

Wilkinson, B. (1998). *Coping with the dangers of tattooing, body piercing and branding.* New York, NY: The Rosen Publishing Group.

Witmer, D. F. & Katzman, S. L. (1997). Online smiles: Does gender make a difference in the use of graphic accents? *Journal of Computer-Mediated Communication, 2*(4).

Xu, S. H. & Rutledge, A. L. (2003). Chicken starts with ch! Kindergartners learn through environmental print. *YC Young Children, 58*(2). 44–51.

Yale University Library. (2007). *What is netiquette? Staff training.* Retrieved February 29, 2008, from http://www.library.yale.edu/training/netiquette/.

Yamada, M. (2000). *Japanese tattooing from the past to the present.* Retrieved March 10, 2008, from http://tattoos.com/mieko.htm.

Young, I. (1997). The Psychohistorical origins of AIDS. In J. Lauritsen and I. Young (Eds), *The AIDS Cult: Essays on the Gay Health Crisis.* Provincetown: Asklepios.

Yuasa, M., Saito, K., & Mukawa, N. (2006). Emoticons convey emotions without cognition of faces: An fMRI study. *In CHI Extended Abstracts.* (pp. 1565–1570). Retrieved February 4, 2007, from http://portal.acm.org/citation.cfm?id=1125451.1125737.

Zaslow, J. (2005). Moving on: Roadside memorials bring grief closer to home—some say a Little Too Close. *The Wall Street Journal,* Sept. 1, 2005, p. D1.

Zuckerman, M. & Driver, R.E. (1985). Telling lies: Verbal and non-verbal correlates of deception. In A. W. Siegman & S. Feldstein (Eds.), *Multichannel integrations of nonverbal behavior.* Hillsdale, NJ: Erlbaum.